Regeneration
and
Conversion

W. E. Best

BAKER BOOK HOUSE
Grand Rapids, Michigan

Printed in the United States of America

CONTENTS

Part I
Regeneration

Part II
Conversion

Part I
REGENERATION

INTRODUCTION

The religious world is staggering under the influence of a depraved intellectualism which denies God His right to operate, among the peoples of the world, as He pleases. No one can believe in *free will* and *free grace* at the same time. These subjects are as diametrically opposed as light and darkness, heaven and hell, or a holy God and an unholy man. To believe in *free will* dethrones the sovereign God; to believe in *free grace* dethrones depraved man. Who is on the throne in your concept of salvation?

The most familiar chapter in the Bible on the new birth is John, chapter three. Christ uncompromisingly asserted the need of regeneration. *The new birth is absolutely necessary because:* (1) *God is holy.* His holiness gives beauty and honor to all His other attributes. God is essentially holy; therefore, He is immutably holy. If man is to have intercourse with the holy God; he must be regenerated, by the Holy Spirit, and thus become holy in the imputed and imparted righteousness of Jesus Christ. (2) *Man is unholy.* He is corrupt and sinful throughout. Natural man is totally unable to do anything spiritually good. He is dead in sin, and his will is enslaved to his evil nature. Man, by nature, can no more live in the presence of God than he can live on the moon, Mercury, or Neptune. I purposely referred to the moon. Someone may say, "The astronauts lived on the moon." Yes, but they were unable to live without the atmosphere of earth to sustain them; even so, men cannot live in God's presence without possessing the holy atmosphere of heaven. (3) *Jesus Christ died on the cross to save His people.* He did not die in vain. The transgressions He bore were those of His people; the wounds and death He suffered were His. Therefore, Jesus Christ suffered vicariously for unregenerate people the Father had given Him. His substitutionary suffering provided redemption to be applied by the Holy Spirit in regeneration. (4) *The Word of God constantly affirms it.* Unregenerate people are spiritually blind, deaf, dumb, and dead.

In the discourse Jesus Christ had with Nicodemus, He said, ". . . Verily, verily, I say unto thee, Except a man be born again, he cannot see the kingdom of God" (John 3:3). This text is a

3

good starting point for a study of the most important aspect in redemption's application.

Who was Nicodemus? He was both a Pharisee and a ruler of the Jews. (1) "A man of the Pharisees" denotes his *religious profession;* and (2) "a ruler (master) of the Jews" describes his *official position.*

Nicodemus, a Pharisee, was a member of the proudest and most influential religious class in the time of our Lord. The Pharisees rejected the message of John the Baptist. "And all the people that heard him, and the publicans, justified God, being baptized with the baptism of John. But the Pharisees and lawyers rejected the counsel of God against themselves, being not baptized of him" (Luke 7:29,30). John, the Identifier, baptized with the baptism of repentance. The Jews were to identify themselves, in this baptism, with their repentance from sin. His baptism, however, does not imply that baptism preceded repentance. Text and context both prove that repentance is a prerequisite to baptism (Matt. 3:7-12). John's baptism was *in* (not with) water *upon* or *at* repentance (Matt. 3:11). The Greek preposition *en* is not instrumental but local, and denotes the place of baptism— the Jordan river. "Unto (upon or at) repentance" is interpreted in this same manner in Matthew 12:41: ". . . they repented *at* the preaching of Jonas . . ." The Pharisees rejected repentance of sin, the prerequisite of baptism, not the rite of baptism itself.

How could Nicodemus, a master of Israel, refuse the message of John the Baptist? Luke said, concerning John the Baptist (Identifier), ". . . he shall be great in the sight of the Lord, and shall drink neither wine nor strong drink; and he shall be filled with the Holy Ghost, even from his mother's womb. And many of the children of Israel shall he turn to the Lord their God. And he shall go before him in the spirit and power of Elias, to turn the hearts of the fathers to the children, and the disobedient to the wisdom of the just; to make ready a people prepared for the Lord" (Luke 1:15-17). Please observe the last phrase of Luke 1:17: "to make ready a people *prepared* for the Lord." If John's mission was only to make ready (or prepare) a people, who were already prepared, then we can understand the reason Nicodemus did not receive John's message. No one will embrace the truth of God until the soil of his heart has been prepared by the Holy Spirit in regeneration. This truth is clearly described in the four soils of Matthew 13. Only the prepared soil received the seed with understanding and brought forth fruit.

The mission of the church *is not to regenerate people;* she is to preach the gospel whereby those, whose hearts have already been prepared in regeneration, are made ready to embrace Christ through conversion. Here is a lesson for all of God's servants to heed. The gospel is good news to those whom the Holy Spirit has regenerated. Paul said it is foolishness to everyone else. "For Christ sent me not to baptize, but to preach the gospel: not with wisdom of words, lest the cross of Christ should be made of none effect. For the preaching of the cross is to them that perish foolishness; but unto us which are saved it is the power of God" (I Cor. 1:17,18).

Nicodemus was a ruler of the Jews, not a mere master of a synagogue. As a member of the Sanhedrin, he was in charge of interpretation and enforcement of the law. A member of this ecclesiastical organization must be highly trained in judical administration. Proof of this is revealed in John 7:50,51: "Nicodemus saith unto them, (he that came to Jesus by night, being one of them,) Doth our law judge any man, before it hear him, and know what he doeth?"

Ecclesiastical affiliation is no insurance against deception. Not only were the Jews deceived in the presence of Christ, but they were beguiled with the Old Testament Scriptures in their hands. This proves that the most likely place to be deceived is in professing Christendom. The presence of the Holy Spirit, in regeneration, is the only guard against deception concerning the Person of Christ.

Why did Nicodemus come to the Lord by night? It is evident that he did not come because he possessed disposition of heart for the Person of Christ. Even though he recognized Jesus Christ as a teacher come from God, he was concerned about his own reputation before the Sanhedrim. The Lord Jesus had already provoked opposition from the ecclesiastics by His assumption of Messianic authority. "And the Jews' passover was at hand, and Jesus went up to Jerusalem, And found in the temple those that sold oxen and sheep and doves, and the changers of money sitting: And when he had made a scourge of small cords, he drove them all out of the temple, and the sheep, and the oxen; and poured out the changers' money, and overthrew the tables; And said unto them that sold doves, Take these things hence; make not my Father's house an house of merchandise. And his disciples remembered that it was written, The zeal of thine house hath eaten me up" (John 2:13-17). Nicodemus came by night because the friendship of the world is enmity with God, whether it is religious or political. James said, "Ye adulterers and adulteresses, know ye not that the friendship of the world is enmity with God? whosoever therefore will be a friend of the world is the enemy of God" (Jas. 4:4).

The conviction of Nicodemus was based on the miracles of Christ, not His Person. He had been convinced in the same manner as those who believed in John 2:23-25, but Jesus Christ would not commit Himself unto them because He knew what was in their hearts. "Now when he was in Jerusalem at the passover, in the feast day, many believed in his name, when they saw the miracles which he did. But Jesus did not commit himself unto them, because he knew all men, and needed not that any should testify of man: for he knew what was in man." The Lord Jesus knows trees by their roots, but we comprehend the character of trees only by their fruit. Man, therefore, looks on the outward appearance; but God sees and knows the heart.

Nicodemus, a man of the Pharisees, was drawn to Christ by an *imperfect faith built upon miracles*. He was in a position where he could not compromise himself in the eyes of the Jewish Sanhedrin. The imperfection of his faith is revealed by his secret coming to Jesus Christ. He manifested courtesy in the manner he addressed the Lord, but so do most religionists as long as they are not personally affected in their religion. The modernists and liberals all speak well of Jesus Christ as teacher. They all have complimentary remarks about His life and influence; but to spiritually minded people, such recognition and praise of the Saviour are insulting rather than complimentary.

Professing Christendom is filled with people, like Nicodemus, whose source of conviction is in the works of Jesus Christ. Such conviction stops short of the Lord's blessed Person. Satan's greatest work is performed in the realm of religion. He magnifies Scriptures that are related to the physical because he knows what carnal minds desire. But he wants nothing to do with Christ. In fact, the man possessed with an unclean spirit, cried out, "Saying,

Let us alone; what have we to do with thee, thou Jesus of Nazareth? art thou come to destroy us? I know thee who thou art, the Holy One of God" (Mark 1:24). Scriptures teach that people are deceived not only in the presence of the Lord with Bibles in their hands, but they shall also call Jesus Christ, Lord. The Lord Jesus said, "Not every one that saith unto me, Lord, Lord, shall enter into the kingdom of heaven; but he that doeth the will of my Father which is in heaven. Many will say to me in that day Lord, Lord, have we not prophesied in thy name? and in thy name have cast out devils? and in thy name done many wonderful works? And then will I profess unto them, I never knew you: depart from me, ye that work iniquity" (Matt. 7:21-23).

Miracles alone will not produce saving faith. The great deceiver of souls gives power to perform "signs and wonders" for the purpose of deception. Egypt's magicians were able, to a certain degree, to duplicate the miracles of Moses. The magicians, who withstood Moses, are named by Paul. "Now as Jannes and Jambres withstood Moses, so do these also resist the truth: men of corrupt minds, reprobate concerning the faith" (II Tim. 3:8). A counterfeit miracle is a "lying wonder and sign" (II Thess. 2:9). Its object is to teach and accredit a lie. Thus, Jannes and Jambres imitated, as far as possible, the miracles of Moses. Just as these deceivers withstood Moses, so do the self-loving and pleasure-seeking professors of Christianity *resist the truth*. They would not think of being without a form of godliness because this is the best way to cover their deception. Paul warns against such false apostles. "For such are false apostles, deceitful workers, transforming themselves into the apostles of Christ. And no marvel; for Satan himself is transformed into an angel of light" (II Cor. 11:13, 14). Depraved man must look, not to miracles but to the grace of God for saving faith. "For by grace are ye saved through faith; and that not of yourselves: it is the gift of God" (Eph. 2:8).

The mere fact that a teacher works wonders and signs is no proof that he is *come from God*. The commendation by Nicodemus was not so complimentary after all, since *lying wonders and signs* were performed by false teachers.

There is great danger of one being misled by the sound of certain Biblical expressions, without understanding their true meaning. I shall give several examples: (1) The Scriptures represent God as omnipotent, yet there are some things He cannot do. He cannot lie, be deceived, or go back on His promise. Omnipotence, therefore, does not mean that God can do everything; but He can do all that does not involve self-contradiction. (2) The Word of God states that Jesus Christ, in dying for His people, took their infirmities, and bare their sicknesses (Matt. 8:17). All that some sincere, but deceived, souls see in this verse is that Jesus Christ carried all the physical infirmities of people into His Calvary experience. Thus, their concept of physical healing is as faulty as their view of spiritual healing. If Jesus Christ stood in the place of the sick, as He stood in the place of the sinner, our sicknesses would be as far removed from us as our sins. Christ's atoning work is absolutely perfect and finished—Godward—so that He is the propitiation for our sins, but its application to our bodies remains yet to be accomplished (II Cor. 4:16; Rom. 8:23; Phil. 3:21). (3) The Bible says that God was in Christ reconciling the world unto Himself (II Cor. 5:19), while the same Book declares there are many appointed to eternal destruction. Thus, all men of the world are not reconciled to God. Only believers are reconciled to God. (4) God's Word says that Christ died for all; it also states that He died for only some—His church, His people, His sheep. That all men have received some benefit from the death of Christ cannot be denied. His death has served as a dam, or barrier, to hold back God's wrath. God's longsuffering is the barrier, but it is salvation to those for whom Christ died (II Pet. 3:9,15). (5) The Word of God invites men to come to Jesus Christ; but the Bible nowhere implies that natural man, unaided and undrawn, can come to Christ. These are only a few examples of Scriptures often misunderstood.

We must be on guard lest we be deceived by the *sound* of Scripture quotations instead of seeking their sense. Every true minister is like Ezra, who read the Word distinctly, gave the sense (the meaning), and caused the people to understand (Neh. 8:8). You might ask, How did Ezra cause the people to understand? In the same manner as John the Baptist made ready a people, whose hearts had already been prepared, to embrace the coming Saviour (Luke 1:17).

Nicodemus, an interpreter of the law, knew that miracles would be associated with the kingdom. The Jews expected that miracles would be wrought by the Messiah, and many had believed in Him on this account (John 2:23-25; 6:14; 7:31). Nicodemus was no exception. He, too, believed and therefore said, ". . . Rabbi, we know that thou art a teacher come from God: for no man can do these miracles that thou doest, except God be with him" (John 3:2). The kingdom shall be permeated with a power, which is above nature, and shall make nature itself promote God's Divine purpose. Miracles are so related to the kingdom that they cannot be separated from it without mutual invalidation. The kingdom is represented, by Jesus Christ, as associated with miracles. He said, "But if I cast out devils by the Spirit of God, then the kingdom of God is come upon you" (Matt. 12:28). The kingdom came, therefore, *unto the Jews* in the manifested power and Person of the Messiah. But the Lord Jesus censured them and predicted their continual and increasing fall. Luke said, ". . . Behold, this child is set for the fall and rising again of many in Israel: and for a sign which shall be spoken against" (Luke 2:34).

"Rabbi" was a title of respect conferred on Jewish teachers. Our Saviour forbade His disciples to wear this title. "But be not ye called Rabbi: for one is your Master, even Christ; and all ye are brethren" (Matt. 23:8). The title was proper for Jesus Christ because He was the great Teacher—the Teacher of all teachers. "Rabbi" literally signifies *great*, and the Lord Jesus Christ is the greatest of the great. It behooves the servants of Christ to be bathed in the Lord's greatness, rather than immersed in the so-called greatness of man. Nicodemus did not see Jesus Christ as the true Messiah, the eternal Son of the eternal Father; he saw Him as only a teacher sent from God. The knowledge of Christ, as the Son of the living God, is the revelation of God. This is something more than flesh and blood can reveal (Matt. 16:16,17). Nicodemus was unable to see any further than the manhood of Jesus Christ, a teacher come from God.

Nicodemus was not entirely insensitive to the works of Christ. The Bible does not teach that all unregenerate men are completely insensitive to the things of God. They may be sensible of the evil of sin with regard to themselves, but do not recognize that it is against God. Damnation may scare them, but pollution does not. Hell may frighten them, but offending God does not disturb them. Agrippa said, "Almost thou persuadest me to be a Christian" (Act 26:28). The prophet Ezekiel spoke about those who come as God's people, sit as they sit, and talk about the message as a lovely song (Ezek. 33:30-33). Nicodemus, an unregenerate man, was attracted to the miracles of a teacher sent from God.

The coming of an unregenerate man, Nicodemus, to Christ is a significant fact that should not be overlooked; but, let me emphasize that it must be studied in the light of its context. His coming was a physical act, brought about by God's providence, the outcome of which was unknown to himself. This physical act must not be confused with coming to Christ for salvation, which is the inward drawing of the Father. His natural ability enabled him to go where Jesus Christ was, but his spiritual inability kept him from recognizing the blessed Person of the eternal Son of God.

Jesus Christ replied to the statement made by Nicodemus, saying, ". . . Verily, verily, I say unto thee, Except a man be born again, he cannot see the kingdom of God" (John 3:3). The true value of Christ's work cannot be known by natural man. Until one is born again, he is unable to recognize the merit of Christ's life and death.

"Verily, verily" is an expression of strong affirmation, denoting *certainty* and *importance* of what Christ was about to say. This double oath of affirmation is used twenty-five times by our Lord, and is recorded by the apostle John alone. Each time this assertion is followed by, "I say unto you." Thus, our Lord gives absolute assurance that His Word can be trusted. The word is really "Amen." Paul said, "For all the promises of God in him are yea, and in him Amen, unto the glory of God by us" (II Cor. 1:20). The "yea" of established truth is in Jesus Christ. Christianity is not imagination but revelation. Therefore, when truth is revealed to the mind and heart of a regenerated individual, his response will be the "Amen" of faith.

The reason this double affirmation, "Verily, verily," is found in John's gospel only is understandable, since John presents Christ as God. The sovereign God assures us of the fulfillment of redemption's application to His chosen ones by prefacing the subject of the new birth with such strong verification. The Lord Jesus is worthy of our fullest confidence; therefore, the enlightened mind does not doubt the fulfillment of His eternal purpose.

Regeneration is necessary in order for one to see further than the flesh. "Except a man be born again, he cannot *see.* . . ." Some, after the presentation of God's message of the gospel, say, "I just do not see it." If they have not been regenerated, then they are telling the truth. Are you going to become angry with them because God has not opened their eyes to behold spiritual things? You may use all human persuasion possible, but you cannot give spiritual life where death reigns. God alone, by a creative act, can bring life out of death.

The sinner is not dying; he is spiritually dead. Every faculty of his being is completely ruined. He cannot *see* (John 3:3), *understand* (I Cor. 2:14), *receive* (John 14:17), *come* (John 6:44), *cease from sin* (II Pet. 2:14), *call* (I Cor. 12:3; Rom. 10:9,10,13), *please God* (Heb. 11:6), or *enter* the kingdom (John 3:5). Man's only hope of spiritual life is in the life-giving power of God's Spirit. Spiritual arguments to an unregenerate man are only warm clothes to a corpse. Debating in this manner is like standing before Lincoln's Memorial and talking to the statute of the former president about moon trips.

External influences neither help nor hinder regeneration. Nicodemus is an example of the former, and Rahab, the harlot, is typical of the latter. God's sovereignty, revealed in regeneration, is seen all through the Scriptures. He is viewed as passing by the rich man, who fared sumptuously every day; and bestowing salvation on Lazarus, who begged at the rich man's table (Luke 16:19-25). God bestows salvation on some who have been brought up under the most advantageous conditions of piety, and on others without any religious training. We read of Godly Hezekiah, the son of wicked Ahaz (II Kings 16); but on the contrary, Scriptures present wicked Absolom, the son of righteous David (II Sam. 15). The only answer to God's sovereign actions is His desire to glorify Himself. Since God glorified His power, justice, and love in the exercise of them; He magnifies His sovereignty in the exercise of His absolute sovereignty. Paul said, "For ye see your calling, brethren, how that not many wise men after the flesh, not many mighty, not many noble, are called: But God hath chosen the foolish things of the world to confound the wise; and God hath chosen the weak things of the world to confound the things which are mighty; And base things of the world, and things which are despised, hath God chosen, yea, and things which are not, to bring to nought things that are: That no flesh should glory in his presence. But of him are ye in Christ Jesus, who of God is made unto us wisdom, and righteousness, and sanctification, and redemption:

That, according as it is written, He that glorieth, let him glory in the Lord" (I Cor. 1:26-31).

The new birth, contrary to what is commonly taught, is something done not merely *for* but *in* man, by the power of the Holy Spirit. Some believe that the subject is active in the new birth, and the Spirit employs the Word as God's means of accomplishing regeneration. But the subject, according to Scripture, is spiritually dead, blind, deaf, and dumb. Thus, the sinner is passive, spiritually speaking; but he is actively engaged in sinful acts. If he cannot cease from sin (II Pet. 2:14), then he is filled with all unrighteousness. He not only commits things worthy of death, but has pleasure in those who perform such evil deeds (Rom. 1:29-32). The Holy Spirit, therefore, must quicken the passive spirit of the sinner making him sensitive to the call of the gospel. Sensitivity to the gospel is the fruit of regeneration. Scriptures classify this as conversion. Conversion will be the subject of study in John 3:14-16. Since the Bible is an orderly Book, we must consider things in their proper order.

REGENERATION PRESUPPOSES DEPRAVITY

Man's inability to recover himself is vividly portrayed in Ezekiel 16. The helpless infant, exposed in the field, would die without help from some other source. Israel is represented under the figure of a woman, who was taken when she was a forsaken and helpless baby, made vulnerable to the vultures of the world. The Lord found her in her own blood—her natural, lost condition. He entered into covenant for Israel, and made her His own.

The covenant preceded Israel's deliverance, just as God's choice of His own in Christ Jesus precedes the provision and application of redemption. The reason religionists frown upon this fact is because it dethrones them as gods. The statement, "We need to let God be God in our lives" is ridiculous. What is man? Is he a god greater than the God of creation, providence, and redemption? Christians should be afraid of anyone who thinks unworthy thoughts about God. David said, "What is man, that thou art mindful of him? . . ." (Ps. 8:4). It has been said that man is nothing more than a little air and dust tempered together, a pile of dust and puff of wind with no solidity in either.

God's eternal purpose is ridiculed by uninformed people. Some advocate, with fleshly fervor, that calling precedes God's eternal election. This is as logical as a contractor building a house before he has the plans drawn. Great struggles continue to rage between human conceptions of the Divine decree. We must not, in the discussion of God's order, suppose a transposition of *temporal succession* into the eternity of God's counsel. The concept of succession in God's decree is a clear form of humanization of God. God is eternal; He is pre-temporal, co-temporal, and post-temporal. Therefore, His decree is present and future as well as past. It is with and after its fulfillment as well as before it. "But he is in one mind, and who can turn him? and what his soul desireth, even that he doeth" (Job 23:13). God's order of salvation cannot be broken down into disorder (Eph. 1; Rom. 8).

Nicodemus was acquainted with God's covenant with Israel. He did not recognize his depravity and need of regeneration when he confronted the Saviour. The doctrine of election, like every other doctrine, is not without its misunderstanding and distortion. Nicodemus, as a Pharisee, prided himself in being the seed of Abraham. He was a member of God's covenant people, but they are not all Israel which are of Israel (Rom. 9:6). He felt as many of his forefathers, when they said, ". . . Is not the Lord among us? none evil can come upon us" (Micah 3:11). The same trend of thinking was manifested by many who came to John's baptism. "And think not to say within yourselves, We have Abraham to our father . . ." (Matt. 3:9). The Scriptures do not present election as a way to self-exaltation, but to true humility. God's mercy and justice go together.

Regeneration presupposes depravity. Nicodemus, a teacher of the Jews, was familiar with Old Testament Scriptures. But familiarity, apart from Divine grace, breeds contempt. The language of our Lord was nothing new to him. The change that must take place in his depraved heart was something more than mental; it was to be an inward cleansing by Divine influence. As there was no beauty in the loathsome child of Ezekiel 16, so there was nothing in this religious Pharisee to please the Lord Jesus Christ.

Non-existent spiritual life cannot give being to itself. Light is not brought out of darkness, neither does love come from hate. Every seed bears its own kind. "That which is born of the flesh is flesh; and that which is born of the Spirit is spirit" (John 3:6). A new creature, therefore, cannot be the product of natural power.

The sinner is not regenerated by combined efforts of God and man. There is no "I will if you will" in regeneration. The record states, "And when I passed by thee, and saw thee polluted in thine own blood, I said unto thee when thou wast in thy blood, Live; yea, I said unto thee when thou wast in thy blood, Live" (Ezek. 16:6). God's passing by was not by chance, but according to His own eternal purpose. Who but God could dispense life with a single syllable, "Live." This is a demonstration of God's unsought and free grace. ". . . I am found of them that sought me not . . ." (Is. 65:1). "Blessed is the man whom thou choosest, and causest to approach unto thee . . ." (Ps. 65:4). But some untutored person cries out, "That is national, not individual." The principle is the same, whether it is national or individual. There are many references, however, to personal election if one has a spiritual mind to see them (Eph. 1:4; Matt. 22:14; Luke 18:7; Rom. 8:28,30,33; Col. 3:12; II Thess. 2:13; II Tim. 1:9). Spiritual honesty, which is greatly lacking today, will take this important doctrine, give its meaning, and show how it is used.

Most religionists think sinners take the first step in their salvation, but informed Christians know better. The day of regeneration is solely the time of God's love and power. "Now when I passed by thee, and looked upon thee, behold, thy time was the time of love; and I spread my skirt over thee, and covered thy nakedness; yea, I sware unto thee, and entered into a covenant with thee, saith the Lord God, and thou becamest mine" (Ezek. 16:8). Just for the sake of argument, if sinners did take the first step, they would be like the Roman myth of St. Dennis. It is said that after the head of Dennis had been cut off, he picked it up and walked two thousand miles with his head in his hand. Some wit, when hearing the story, said, "I see no difficulty in the two thousand mile walk. The difficulty lay in the first step."

There was a debate some years ago between a liberal preacher and an evangelical minister. The liberal's subject was entitled, "Fanning the spark into a flame." He taught that there is, in every person, a Divine spark which only needs fanning by good influence and education. "If the spark is given proper attention," he said, "It will burn into a blazing fire of good influence and works." The evangelical minister took the position that there is no Divine spark in natural man. Therefore, his rebuttal was, "There is no spark to fan." At the conclusion of the rebuttal address, the liberal preacher stood up and said, "I commend you on your reply, but I have a question to ask you. Do you believe that man has the ability, in himself, to either accept or reject the gospel?" The evangelical minister, without a moment's hesitation, replied, "Yes, I surely do." The liberal then asked, "What is this ability in man?" The evangelical replied, "That ability is man's free will." Then the liberal smiled and said, "You call it free will, and I call it a spark of goodness." Actually, there was no difference between these men when it came to the subject of man's condition by nature. They both denied depravity, which is essential to the proper concept of regeneration and conversion.

Ability to believe on Jesus Christ is not produced by the fire of man's own kindling. Nicodemus sat in the presence of Jesus Christ, Who was the light of the world, but he knew not his own true condition. Knowledge of spiritual things, in a natural way, only increases blindness. This is the reason Nicodemus asked, ". . . How can a man be born when he is old? can he enter the second time into his mother's womb, and be born?" (John 3:4). Apart from spiritual blindness, this would be hard to understand because "to be born again" was a common expression among the Jews. It denoted a change from Gentileism to Judaism. Now, that the Lord was applying this same expression to the Jews, in fact to every man, it appeared absurd to a religious master of the Jews. The proper question for Nicodemus should have been, "Who can?" Our Lord said, "If thine eye be evil, thy whole body shall be full of darkness. If therefore the light that is in thee be darkness, how great is that darkness!" (Matt. 6:22,23).

Nicodemus sat in subjective, not objective darkness. There is a twofold darkness: *Objective* and *Subjective*. This word is a metaphorical expression borrowed from that which is natural. It is the absence of light. (1) *Objective darkness* consists in the want of those means whereby men may be enlightened in the knowledge of God (Ps. 19:7-11; 119:105; II Pet. 1:19). Paul was indebted, therefore, to take the light of the gospel to Rome, "I am debtor both to the Greeks, and to the Barbarians; both to the wise, and to the unwise. So, as much as in me is, I am ready to preach the gospel to you that are at Rome also" (Rom. 1:14,15). The work of the Holy Spirit is needed to dispel this condition. Hence, Paul was sent, by the Holy Spirit, for the purpose of dispelling objective darkness (Acts 16:6-13). As in darkness we can see nothing, so those who are ignorant of God are said to be in darkness. Christ said, "The people which sat in darkness saw great light . . ." (Matt. 4:16). (2) *Subjective darkness* is that of the unregenerate. The light shines in darkness, but the darkness comprehends it not (John 1:5). This was the position of Nicodemus. Whatever light men might have by nature, or may gather from the book of creation, will not enable them to comprehend the light of God shining in the face of His Son. "For God, who commanded the light to shine out of darkness, hath shined in our hearts, to give the light of the knowledge of the glory of God in the face of Jesus Christ" (II Cor. 4:6). Subjective darkness can be dispersed only by the work of the Spirit in regeneration and calling, ". . . called you out of darkness into . . . light" (I Pet. 2:9). "For ye were sometimes darkness, but now are ye light in the Lord . . ." (Eph. 5:8). The regenerated and called person, ". . . shall not walk in darkness, but shall have the light of life" (John 8:12). Nicodemus did not need objective light. Subjective light in regeneration, which he must possess in order to see the kingdom, was his need.

REGENERATION PRECEDES THE
SANCTIFYING-INFLUENCE OF THE GOSPEL

The new birth is not accomplished by preaching the gospel. Gospel light held no more attraction to Nicodemus than the light of the sun to a blind man. The good news of Christ's Person and work is spiritual, but the natural man cannot understand spiritual things, ". . . the natural man receiveth not the things of the Spirit of God: for they are foolishness unto him: neither can he know them, because they are spiritually discerned" (I Cor. 2:14). Nicodemus' spiritual destitution was manifested in his question, ". . . How can a man be born when he is old? can he enter the second time into his mother's womb, and be born?" (John 3:4). This proves that he was yet a natural man. Our Lord did not satisfy his curiosity; but stressed, in reply, the absolute necessity of being born again.

Regeneration precedes the sanctifying influence of the gospel. This is necessary to render the light of gospel truth effective. What is the good news to a dead man? As light cannot restore sight to a blind man, so the light of the gospel cannot give spiritual light to one who is spiritually blind.

Some earnestly maintain that life is in the seed of the Word. They use Hebrews 4:12 as their proof text: "For the word of God is quick, and powerful, and sharper than any two-edged sword, piercing even to the dividing asunder of soul and spirit, and of the joints and marrow, and is a discerner of the thoughts and intents of the heart." This verse cannot be properly ascribed to the word of the gospel. The *word of the gospel* is the instrumental means of conversion, not regeneration. In the light of the context of Hebrews 4:12, the Word could refer to none other than Jesus Christ. The exhortation is based upon His infinite understanding, "Neither is there any creature that is not manifest in his sight: but all things are naked and opened unto the eyes of him with whom we have to do" (Heb. 4:13). The all-seeing eye of Jesus Christ, not the word of the gospel, penetrates every thought and action of man. Jesus Christ, the incarnate Word (Rev. 19:13), is the Person to Whom the Hebrew believers must give an account of their profession of faith and obedience. The attributes of *living*, *powerful*, and *discerning* are attributed to the Lord Jesus Christ. The word of the gospel is *living* (John

6:63; I Pet. 1:23), but the word of preaching cannot discern the human heart. This is a prerogative that belongs to the Persons of the Godhead. Only the prepared soil, according to Matthew 13:1-9, understands and bears fruit. Such preparation is accomplished, by the Holy Spirit, in regeneration.

Although light cannot restore sight to the blind or heal the diseased organ of sight, it is essential to every exercise of the power of vision. Without objective truth, concerning the Person and Work of Jesus Christ, regenerated Nicodemus would remain in darkness. But that is not the subject of John 3:1-13. That will be the topic that shall form the basis of the study of John 3:13-18. The word of the gospel is powerful; it *convinces, converts,* and *sanctifies* the regenerated mind and heart. But, just as the Lord gave the apostles power to work miracles, a power not in themselves; so the Lord has given the word of truth, yet the power of God is not in the written word itself.

One of the greatest blunders, on the subject of the new birth, is to make it dependent on man's faith. Opposers of Biblical regeneration advocate the new birth must, in some way, be the response of one who hears the gospel. Such verses as, James 1:18 and I Peter 1:23, are used to prove their theory; but the exegesis of the two texts demands no such conclusion. James 1:18 does not refer to begetting or conception, but bringing forth or giving birth. Immediate regeneration does not deny that the new birth, in which the new life becomes manifest, is secured by response to the gospel; but distinction must be made between conception and birth. They are not the same. There are two prepositions, in I Peter 1:23, that must be distinguished before the verse can be understood. The first is *"of (ek—*from out of—the source) incorruptible seed."* This is not the instrument, but the source of regeneration. *"By (dia—*through—the instrument) the word of God"* is the second; this shows that God's word is the instrument of conversion, not regeneration.

God's act of giving life, to those who are spiritually dead, is distinct from the gospel; just as the faculty of sight is different from light. Quickening is an immediate and creative act, "And you hath he quickened, who were dead in trespasses and sins" (Eph. 2:1). No instrumental means are used with God's creative act. The word does not produce life, but it is effective in those who possess life. Life is responsive to living things. Nicodemus was told that he had to be born again before he could see. Once the faculty of sight is given; the recipient is guided, by the word, to repentance and faith.

Our Lord first mentioned the new birth before He told Nicodemus to believe. Faith, that embraces Jesus Christ in salvation, is the fruit of regeneration. But, does not faith come by hearing, and hearing by the word of truth? The ministry of the word effects conversion and sanctification, but the word itself does not effect regeneration. It does not unstop deaf ears and open blind eyes. Scripture teaches that faith comes by hearing (Rom. 10:17), but this faith is not of man. Saving faith is the gift of God (Eph. 2:8; Phil. 1:29; Heb. 12:2). Distinction must be made between the faculty of faith and its exercise. (1) The *faculty of faith* (ability to embrace Christ in a spiritual manner) is implanted in man's heart in regeneration. This is the immediate (without means) and sovereign work of the Spirit. (2) The *exercise of faith* is wrought in conversion and sanctification by the power of indwelling life.

God's servants, in witnessing, are to beseech men to believe the gospel. But does this not contradict what has just been stated by Christ in His discourse with Nicodemus? No, it does not. The Lord knew that Nicodemus had not been born again; Christians, however, cannot know whether or not a man is born again because they do not see his heart. Therefore, their exhortation is for people to believe on the Lord Jesus Christ. When someone asks, "What must I do to be saved?"; the answer should be, "Believe on the Lord Jesus Christ and thou shalt be saved . . ." (Acts 16:31).

The word of God is very clear in its manner of presenting the truth of the gospel to sinners. "For whosoever shall call upon the name of the Lord shall be saved. How then shall they call on him in whom they have not believed? and how shall they believe in him of whom they have not heard? and how shall they hear without a preacher?" (Rom. 10:13,14). Four words stand out in these verses: call, believe, heard, and preacher. (1) They cannot *call* on Christ in whom they have not *believed*. (2) They are unable to believe in him of whom they have never *heard*. Who unstops deaf ears? "The *hearing ear*, and the *seeing eye*, the Lord hath made even both of them" (Prov. 20:12). Ability to hear does not originate with either the spoken word or the preacher; it is the sovereign work of God. (3) The *preacher* is God's ordained means of conversion, not regeneration. "For Christ sent me not to baptize, but to preach the gospel: not with wisdom of words, lest the cross of Christ should be made of none effect. For the preaching of the cross is to them that perish foolishness; but unto us which are saved it is the power of God . . . For after that in the wisdom of God the world by wisdom knew not God, it pleased God by the foolishness of preaching to save them that believe" (I Cor. 1:17, 18,21). The power of preaching comes from neither the spoken word nor the preacher, but from the Spirit of God, whose instrument it is. "And take the helmet of salvation, and the sword of the Spirit, which is the word of God" (Eph. 6:17). The word taken abstractly, separated from the soil of the human heart, is called "foolishness of preaching" (I Cor. 1:21). The excellency of God's power is of God, not of His ministers. "But we have this treasure in earthen vessels, that the excellency of the power may be of God, and not of us" (II Cor. 4:7). Ministers are nothing, in a comparative sense, when it comes to effecting the increase of God. "I have planted, Apollos watered; but God gave the increase. So then neither is he that planteth anything, neither he that watereth; but God that giveth the increase" (I Cor.3:6,7). What are trumpets if no breath is breathed into them, and what are preachers if they are not indwelt and empowered to preach the gospel of truth?

The necessity of the new birth is the natural consequence of man's depravity. Thus, to *see* and *enter* the kingdom, man must be born again. As we have proved that the hearing ear is of God, so we shall now establish the fact that the seeing eye is also of God. Christ said to blind Nicodemus, ". . . Verily, verily, I say unto thee, Except a man be born again, he cannot see the kingdom of God" (John 3:3). Nicodemus' spiritual blindness was manifested by his question," . . . How can a man be born when he is old? can he enter the second time into his mother's womb, and be born?" (John 3:4).

Spiritual blindness is attributed to the *nature of sin*, not to the sin of nature. We have a Biblical example of this in John, chapter nine. Our Lord had been driven from the temple by His enemies. "And as Jesus passed by, he saw a man which was blind from his birth. And his disciples asked him, saying, Master, who did sin, this man, or his parents, that he was born blind? Jesus answered, Neither hath this man sinned, nor his parents: but that the works of God should be made manifest in him" (John 9:1-3). The meaning of these words is not to be taken from what appears on the surface. Our Lord was not teaching that neither this man, nor his parents, had ever sinned. Scripture states that all men have sinned and come short of God's glory (Rom. 3:23), but the Lord was telling the disciples that this man was not being punished for actual sin committed by either him or his parents. It should be remembered, that the *nature of sin* is the fountain from which all afflictions and acts of sin flow. This particular case of blindness was ordained of God, for the manifestation of His glory and mercy, not for any particular sin committed. All men are, by nature, spiritually blind; but if men had their just punishment, they would all be physically blind. Only an act of mercy prevents all from being born physically blind. The complaint should not be why this man was born blind, but why were any of us born with physical sight? It has been said that sentences of providence are very long, and we must read a great way before we shall understand.

It is vain to say that men are regenerated by the power of the gospel. The brightness of the noonday sun has no effect on a blind man any more than the flickering of a match. Nicodemus stood in the presence of not only *Incarnate* but *spoken* truth. He saw neither the Person of Jesus Christ, nor the truth of what He was saying. "But we speak the widsom of God in a mystery, even the hidden wisdom, which God ordained before the world unto our glory: Which none of the princes of this world knew: for had they known it, they would not have crucified the Lord of glory. But as it is written, Eye hath not seen, nor ear heard, neither have entered into the heart of man, the things which God hath prepared for them that love him. But God hath revealed them unto us by his Spirit: for the Spirit searcheth all things, yea, the deep things of God" (I Cor. 2:7-10).

REGENERATION IS A NECESSITY

Seeing and entering the kingdom must be preceded by regeneration. The kingdom, in John 3:3,5, is not soteriological (the science of salvation). When Nicodemus was perplexed about the way of entrance into the kingdom, the Lord's reply was a *rebuke* rather than a **definition**. ". . . Art thou a master of Israel, and knowest not these things?" (John 3:10). This rebuke makes no sense without assuming that the kingdom announced was the kingdom of Old Testament prophecy. The Lord appealed to Nicodemus on the basis that he ought to know these things, evidently, because they were recorded in the Old Testament Scriptures. Sprinkling with "clean water," obtaining of the "new spirit," and "raising of the dead" are all represented as essential to the introduction of the kingdom and its blessings.

Regeneration qualifies a person for the kingdom. Through regeneration and conversion, the believer becomes an *heir* of the kingdom, "Hearken, my beloved brethren, Hath not God chosen the poor of this world rich in faith, and heirs of the kingdom which he hath promised to them that love him?" (Jas. 2:5). An heir is one who is entitled to something promised. Heirship is the consequence of faith, and faith is the fruit of election. Election to grace is signified in faith, and predestination to glory is denoted in heirship (Rom. 8:29). The believer, through much suffering, shall enter into the kingdom (Acts 14:22). This kingdom cannot fail because it was prepared for the heir from the foundation of the world (Matt. 25:34).

The kingdom is sure to all believers, whether in heaven or on earth. The realization of this blessed experience, however, must wait for the second coming of Jesus Christ in glory. The patriarchs all died in faith, not having received the promise (Heb. 11:39,40); but having seen it afar off, they were persuaded of its ultimate fulfillment (Heb. 11:13).

How did the patriarchs see the kingdom afar off? Through the eye of faith because faith is the substance of things hoped for, the evidence of things not seen. Nicodemus, in the same manner, would be able to *see* the kingdom as his inheritance. Thus, *seeing*, by faith, precedes *entering* the kingdom. Nicodemus could never expect to enter the kingdom, though he was of the natural seed of

Abraham, except by the new birth. Regeneration would make him an heir of the kingdom, and then enable him to see it by faith.

Knowledge of religious subjects may be possessed apart from regeneration. It cannot be denied that Nicodemus had some knowledge of the kingdom, but his question concerning the new birth proves that he lacked grace. His ignorance of regeneration, however, does not alter the meaning of the kingdom in Old Testament prophecy.

The kingdom of Christ will be different from, both His control of the church as her Head and His sovereign providential rule over the universe. If the kingdom of prophecy were in existence now, the knowledge of the Lord would cover the earth as the waters cover the sea. Christ's reign in the kingdom will be visible; His Headship of the church and His sovereign action in providence are both invisible. The world knows nothing about Headship and Sovereignty, and this age could care less about what God is doing. The time will come, however, when all shall acknowledge the Lordship of Christ Jesus. This will be when He reigns visibly on the earth (Phil. 2:9-11).

Those who believe the kingdom should be interpreted eschatologically are accused of carnalizing that which should be spiritual. Such charge makes as much sense as saying the human nature of Jesus Christ detracts from the spirituality of His Person. The kingdom, when it is established, will be thoroughly spiritual.

Jesus Christ, in answering the question of Nicodemus as to *how* the new birth takes place, repeats the necessity of regeneration. "Jesus answered, Verily, verily, I say unto thee, Except a man be born of water and of the Spirit, he cannot enter into the kingdom of God" (John 3:5). Baptismal regeneration is as far removed from this text as hell is from heaven. There is as much similarity between regeneration (the immediate work of the Spirit in the soul) and baptismal regeneration (the mediate work of man by the use of water), as there is between light and darkness. If it were not for the heresy applied to this verse, there would be no need for such discussion. But when willful and persistent distortion of a verse continues, it behooves the man of God to expose the evil doctrine. Many illustrations of such exposure are seen throughout the Scripture. "The prophets prophesy falsely, and the priests bear rule by their means; and my people love to have it so: and what will ye do in the end thereof?" (Jer. 5:31). False prophets and teachers are called *reprobate silver* because the Lord has rejected them (Jer. 6:30). As there is no real value in reprobate silver, so there is no spiritual value in false teachers. "But though we, or an angel from heaven, preach any other gospel unto you than that which we have preached unto you, let him be accursed. As we said before, so say I now again, If any man preach any other gospel unto you than that ye have received, let him be accursed" (Gal. 1:8,9). "I would they were even cut off which trouble you" (Gal. 5:12).

In refuting the heresy of baptismal regeneration, there must be a distinction between *birth* and *burial*. Regeneration is a birth, but baptism is a burial. ". . . buried with him by baptism into death: that like as Christ was raised up from the dead . . . so we also should walk in newness of life" (Rom. 6:4). Now, the question is, was our Lord talking about regeneration (new birth) or burial (baptism) ? The context proves to every enlightened mind and heart, that the new birth is the subject of John 3:1-10.

It is commonly questioned, by those who believe in baptismal regeneration, "If Jesus did not mean water, why did He say water?" The reply is, "If our Lord meant baptism, why did He not say baptism?" Christ did not say, "Except you be *baptized of (ek) water*" in this verse. A repentant person is said to be baptized *in (en) water* (Matt. 3:11). Baptism is never expressed by water only, without some additional words to show that the ordinance of baptism is intended (John 4:2; Acts 2:38-41; 8:36,37; 9:18; 10:44-48).

Water, in a baptistry or font, is as impotent to regenerate man as the water in Jacob's well. "Jesus answered and said unto her, Whosoever drinketh of this water shall thirst again: But whosoever drinketh of the water that I shall give him shall never thirst; but the water that I shall give him shall be in him a well of water springing up into everlasting life" (John 4:13,14). Life-giving water, according to John 4:14, is the gift of God. There are four things we must observe about this gift of life-giving water: (1) The *Giver*—"I shall give him." (2) The *Habitation*—"The water that I shall give him shall be *in him*." Hence, it is internal, not external. (3) The *Function*—"a well of water *springing up*." Conversion experiences arise from the indwelling principle of life. (4) The *Purpose*—"into *everlasting life*." The difference between grace and glory may not be as great as one might imagine.

The nature of both is the same. Grace is glory in the bud; glory is grace in the flower. The Christian, therefore, has something of heaven now. God purifies the streams by regenerating the fountain.

We are told that baptism does not put away the filth of the flesh. "By which also he went and preached unto the spirits in prison; Which sometime were disobedient, when once the long-suffering of God waited in the days of Noah, while the ark was preparing, wherein few, that is, eight souls were saved by water. The like figure whereunto even baptism doth also now save us (not the putting away of the filth of the flesh, but the answer of a good conscience toward God,) by the resurrection of Jesus Christ" (I Pet. 3:19-21). The new birth, therefore, is not an outward washing, but an inward cleansing by the Holy Spirit. It is the washing of regeneration. "Not by works of righteousness which we have done, but according to his mercy he saved us, by the washing of regeneration, and renewing of the Holy Ghost" (Titus 3:5). Regeneration is an *inward* work of grace; baptism is an *outward* work of man. Regeneration is the inward and immediate work of the Spirit; baptism is the mediate symbol of inward cleansing, applied externally. Christ said, ". . . the water that I shall give him shall be in him a well of water springing up into everlasting life" (John 4:14). The water of baptism is not water that shall be *in* man; neither is it water that brings everlasting life or salvation. How can the heart of man be cleansed by the outward sign of baptism?

The religion of most people is only external. The baptismal regenerationist has the same order of religion as the Pharisees. "Woe unto you, scribes and Pharisees, hypocrites! for ye pay tithe of mint and anise and cummin, and have omitted the weightier matters of the law, judgment, mercy and faith: these ought ye to have done, and not to leave the other undone. Ye blind guides, which strain at a gnat, and swallow a camel. Woe unto you, scribes and Pharisees, hypocrites! for ye make clean the outside of the cup and of the platter, but within they are full of extortion and excess. Thou blind Pharisee, cleanse first that which is within the cup and platter, that the outside of them may be clean also. Woe unto you, scribes and Pharisees, hypocrites! for ye are like unto whited sepulchres, which indeed appear beautiful outward, but are within full of dead men's bones, and of all uncleanness" (Matt. 23:23-27). The outward righteousness of man is of no value, until the heart is first made pure. Good works may be produced by a storm of human compulsion, rather than the fruit of a regenerate tree. It is possible to do many things without the heart being in the things accomplished. The order which our Lord gave is quite different. "How much more shall the blood of Christ, who through the eternal Spirit offered himself without spot to God, purge your conscience from dead works to serve the living God?" (Heb. 9:14). "For we are his workmanship, created in Christ Jesus unto good works, which God hath before ordained that we should walk in them" (Eph. 2:10). Thus, *born of water and Spirit* no more means baptismal regeneration; than the eating of Christ's flesh and drinking His blood in John 6:33-58 means transubstantiation, in the Lord's Supper.

Regeneration is accomplished by neither natural power nor external ordinances. As Abraham was justified through faith, apart from circumcision (Rom. 4:10); so the chosen of God are regenerated and justified by God, without any ordinance performed by man.

The Holy Spirit, in performing regeneration, works like water. As the "Holy Ghost and fire" (Matt. 3:11) signify one thing—the purging of dross—in sanctification; so "water and Spirit" (John 3:5) indicate one thing—the Spirit cleansing like water—in regeneration. This expression, concerning the work of the Spirit under the name of water, was not unusual in the Old Testament. "For I will pour water upon him that is thirsty, and floods upon the dry ground: I will pour my spirit upon thy seed, and my blessing upon thine offspring" (Is. 44:3). "Then will I sprinkle clean water upon you, and ye shall be clean: from all your filthiness, and from all your idols, will I cleanse you" (Ezek. 36:25). Hence, it is that Christ repeats only *the Spirit* in verse six, so He includes all that is signified by *water and Spirit* in verse five. "That which is born of the Spirit is spirit" (John 3:6).

Man is, by his natural birth, depraved. "That which is born of the flesh is flesh" (John 3:6). Flesh, in this verse, is not the fleshly part of man. It does not refer to his body, but to his unregenerate nature. The preposition is *of (ek)*, which means source; this is the same as *of corruptible seed* (I Pet. 1:23). Thus, the source of unregenerate nature is unregenerate nature. As Adam begat a son in his own likeness, not God's likeness; so the descendant of Adam begets a son in his own likeness, not the likeness of God. This means that a born again parent begets an unregenerate child. The parent cannot communicate grace, but he does transmit the fallen nature. Salvation, therefore, does not run in the blood stream. "Which were born, not of blood, nor of the will of the flesh, nor of the will of man, but of God" (John 1:13).

The Bible teaches *universal corruption*. "For all have sinned, and come short of the glory of God" (Rom. 3.23). "And you hath he quickened, who were dead in trespasses and sins; Wherein in time past ye walked according to the course of this world, according to the prince of the power of the air, the spirit that now worketh in the children of disobedience: among whom also we all had our conversation in times past in the lusts of our flesh, fulfilling the desires of the flesh and of the mind; and were by nature the children of wrath, even as others" (Eph. 2:1-3). Scripture refers to corruption in various ways. It emphatically states that there is no one, in his natural condition, who has an understanding heart and seeks God. "The Lord looked down from heaven upon the children of men, to see if there were any that did understand, and seek God. They are all gone aside, they are all together become filthy: there is none that doeth good, no, not one" (Ps. 14:2,3). "There is none that understandeth, there is none that seeketh after God" (Rom. 3:11). Regardless of what has been taught, no unregenerate person seeks the Lord. He is always viewed as running and hiding from God. Adam, as soon as he fell in the garden, fled among the trees and sought to hide from God. "And they heard the voice of the Lord God walking in the garden in the cool of the day: and Adam and his wife hid themselves from the presence of the Lord God amongst the trees of the garden" (Gen. 3:8). Isaiah said, "All we like sheep have gone astray . . ." (Is. 53:6). ". . . I was found of *them that sought me not* . . ." (Rom. 10:20)

Man's corruption is evident in every part of his life. His heart is hard and impenitent (Rom. 2:5), and his life is filled with ungodliness and unrighteousness (Rom. 1:18). The sinner is characterized by these things, and this is not something incidental; but filling his whole mind, heart, and life to its utmost depths. Romans 3:9,10 will disarm any suspicion of finding something good in the sinner.

Our Lord, in showing Nicodemus his true condition, points

him to the fact that even in natural things he lacked comprehension. The fall, therefore, caused man's understanding of natural things to have its limitations. In referring to the wind, Christ said, ". . . thou hearest the sound thereof, but canst not tell whence it cometh, and whither it goeth . . ." (John 3:8). The Saviour went on to say, "If I have told you earthly things, and ye believe not, how shall ye believe, if I tell you of heavenly things?" (John 3:12). Job was utterly perplexed by many questions concerning creation (Job 38; 39); but, to the spiritual mind, creation is the *lattice* behind which God hides Himself. "My beloved is like a roe or a young hart: behold, he standeth behind our wall, he looketh forth at the windows, shewing himself through the lattice" (S. of S. 2:9). And, yet, He reveals Himself to faith. "O the depth of the riches both of the wisdom and knowledge of God! how unsearchable are his judgments, and his ways past finding out! For who hath known the mind of the Lord? or who hath been his counsellor?" (Rom. 11:33,34).

The knowledge of man's *depravity* and *redemption* are the two hinges upon which the whole structure of regeneration moves. As the former cannot be understood without apprehending the latter; so the latter cannot be known without a basic knowledge of the former. Here is where the real problem lies. (1) Is man, in his lost condition, totally unable to do anything of a spiritual nature? (2) Is the new birth wholly of God? To say that man, in his unregenerate condition, can repent and believe is to deny depravity. Some ask, "If man cannot do these things, then why is he thus commanded?" A thief's inability to repay what he has stolen does not affect the right of the person he has deprived. Neither does man's inability, because of the fall, affect God's right to command. God, therefore, has the right to command the sinner to repent and believe. However, the sinner has made himself unable to do so by his complicity with Adam in original sin (Rom. 5:12). Each man shall give an account of himself to God.

Redemption is not something provided as an offer for all men; but a redemption made sure to those whom God sovereignly regenerates. Regeneration, therefore, is not a life line thrown out to a drowning man (a drowning man is not dead), but a ransom applied to a person *dead in trespasses and sins*. Do not overlook the fact that both repentance (Jer. 31:18-21; Acts 11:18) and faith (Eph. 2:8; Phil. 1:29; Heb. 12:2) are of God. They are God's gifts of salvation; therefore, cannot be man's contribution to his salvation.

The flesh, or old nature, is not changed in regeneration. It is *condemned*, but not changed in the believer. "For what the law could not do, in that it was weak through the flesh, God sending his own Son in the likeness of sinful flesh, and for sin, condemned sin in the flesh" (Rom. 8:3). Flesh, therefore, either signifies the state of unregenerate man; or flesh in the regenerate, which resists the Spirit. "For the flesh lusteth against the Spirit, and the Spirit against the flesh: and these are contrary the one to the other; so that ye cannot do the things that ye would" (Gal. 5:17). The old nature (flesh) resides in the man, who has been born of God, but it does not reign. Regenerate man does not live in the old nature, but flesh is in the believer. Regeneration does not destroy the presence and power of the flesh in the saint; but it has been *judicially condemned,* in the sacrifice of Jesus Christ.

When one is regenerated, by the Spirit of God, he is a spiritual person. ". . . and that which is born of the Spirit is spirit" (John 3:6). Christ's first reference to "Spirit" is used of the *Author* of the new birth; His second reference to "spirit" is used of the *spiritual life* of the person regenerated.

"Born of *(ek)* the Spirit" proves that the third Person of the Godhead is the One Who applies redemption. If the Holy Spirit were nothing more than an influence, such a creative act could never take place in the soul of a depraved man. A mere influence does not possess inherent power. The Holy Spirit is more than an influence, He is a Divine Person; and , as a Person, He exerts Divine influence. He is called "God," and God is a Person. "But Peter said, Ananias, why hath Satan filled thine heart to lie to the Holy Ghost, and to keep back part of the price of the land? Whiles it remained, was it not thine own? and after it was sold, was it not in thine own power? why hast thou conceived this thing in thine heart? thou hast not lied unto men, but unto God" (Acts 5:3,4).

Spiritual living is the fruit of being born of the Spirit. Hence, the word "spirit" in the latter part of John 3:6 refers to the spiritual nature and its exercise. The spiritual man has a spiritual mind; he is possessed with a Person Who indwells, seals, intercedes, and empowers. Romans eight shows the power of the Spirit to: (1) liberate (vs. 2-4); (2) provide (vs. 5,6); (3) indwell (v. 9); (4) quicken (v. 11); (5) triumph (v. 13); (6) guide (v. 14); (7) deliver from slavish fear (v. 15); (8) give witness to salvation (v. 16); (9) overrule in the affairs of life (v. 26); and (10) search and intercede (v. 27). In I Corinthians 2:10-14, the Holy Spirit reveals (v. 10), teaches (v. 13), discerns (v. 14), and searches (v. 10). But, before leaving these wonderful helps of the Spirit, we must ask, to Whom does the Spirit direct the believer's attention in revealing, teaching, discerning, and searching? The answer is given in John 16:13,14. "Howbeit when he, the Spirit of truth, is come, he will guide you into all truth: for he shall not speak of himself; but whatsoever he shall hear, that shall he speak: and he will shew you things to come. He shall glorify me: for he shall receive of mine, and shall shew it unto you."

Evidence of being born of the Spirit is manifested in *disposition*, *discernment*, and *action* of a believer. He reveals not only the habits, but also the spirit of grace.

Nicodemus' overwhelming astonishment is brought to light by Christ's statement, "Marvel not that I said unto thee, Ye must be born again" (John 3:7). This religious Pharisee was as startled, at the subject of regeneration, as most religionists are today. It was as *new* to his religious mind, as Paul's message was to the Athenians (Act 17:22-31).

Before we proceed in the subject of regeneration proper, we must clear away the debris of religious opinion and terminology. The new birth is not:

1. Experimental. The creative act of the Holy Spirit in the soul is instantaneous; therefore, regeneration takes place in the sphere of the sub-consciousness. Regeneration is compared to conception in the womb, rather than the bringing forth of life in birth. Thus, as conception precedes birth, so regeneration precedes conversion (I John 3:9; I Pet. 1:23). Repentance and faith are a vital part of the new creation (II Cor. 5:17), and that which is a part cannot be the cause of itself.

2. Dependent on repentance and faith. Repentance and faith are the fruit of regeneration, which is the tree. As the fruit does not bear the tree, so repentance and faith do not bear regenera-

tion (Acts 11:18; Eph. 2:8). How can the creative act of God be conditioned on repentance and faith?

3. Contingent on the word of the gospel. There is no more disposition in an unregenerate man to receive the gospel of Christ, than there is in darkness to receive light. The light shines in darkness, and the darkness comprehends it not (John 1:5). A distinction must be made between a creative word or command (Gen. 1:3; Ezek. 16:6), and the word of preaching (I Cor. 1:18-21).

4. Reliant on the sinner taking the first step, by manifesting his willingness to trust Christ. Who can will? Christ said to the unregenerate, "And ye will not come to me, that ye might have life" (John 5:40). Those who have the wrong concept of salvation believe that the will of man is the determining factor, but the will that determines is the same depraved will that must be determined. Disease is in the will; therefore, a diseased will cannot provide a cure. If man has a "free will" to choose good or evil, then why is it that all men choose the evil of free will?

5. Preceded by Divine conviction. The external preaching of the word alone does not effect conviction, that is of God. Divine conviction is related to and inseparable from regeneration. The indwelling Spirit of the regenerate is necessary to apply the external word, or the subjective Spirit is required to apply the objective word (John 16:8-11). David said, "For with thee is the fountain of life: in thy light shall we see light" (Ps. 36:9). Only in the light of the Divine Spirit in regeneration can a person be brought under the power of the light of the gospel (II Tim. 1:10). The Holy Spirit uses the word of truth to convict the regenerate person of the sins of nature, and the nature of sin. The born again man is convicted of his sins, but he is also cognizant of his sinful nature from which those sins issue.

6. Prefaced by the effectual call. Calling may be distinguished from regeneration, yet it is closely associated with it (Rom. 8:28-31; II Thess. 2:13,14; II Pet. 1:10; Matt. 22:14). Calling is the Divine summons, which appeals to the principle of life that causes the will to act. Regeneration occurs independently of understanding, but calling is associated with understanding. Calling, that is effectual, presupposes life. He that is called must

be able to hear and come to Christ, and he is made able in regeneration.

7. Effected by the ordinance of baptism. Baptism is a symbolic picture of the believer's union with Jesus Christ in His death, burial, and resurrection (Rom. 6:3-6; Acts 8:36-38). Baptism, therefore, is a proclaiming but not a procuring ordinance. Blood always precedes water. Since baptism is a *picture,* then how can a picture save? Baptism is the answer of a good conscience (I Pet. 3:21), and the answer must follow the good conscience. Is the conscience made good by: (1) blood only; (2) water only; or (3) blood and water? The answer is found in Hebrews 9:14: "How much more shall the blood of Christ, who through the eternal Spirit offered himself without spot to God, purge your conscience from dead works to serve the living God?" Baptism is *putting on Christ* (Gal. 3:26,27), but only believers are thus commanded (Rom. 13:11-14).

God has never had but one means for man's redemption, and that method is grace. Grace can act only on the foundation that all alike deserve nothing. Therefore, through unmerited favor, grace is bestowed on some. The people of God, in the Old Testament, were the recipients of grace. God's method of salvation was not changed in the New Testament (Eph. 2:8-10). Where does the ordinance of baptism fit into God's purpose of man's deliverance from the bondage of sin? Baptism, which is a New Testament ordinance, has no place in God's message for the sinner's salvation. Paul, a New Testament apostle and preacher (II Tim. 1:11), preached the same message for sanctification through faith that was proclaimed by Moses and the prophets. "But shewed first unto them of Damascus, and at Jerusalem, and throughout all the coasts of Judaea, and then to the Gentiles, that they should repent and turn to God, and do works meet for repentance. For these causes the Jews caught me in the temple, and went about to kill me. Having therefore obtained help of God, I continue unto this day, witnessing both to small and great, saying none other things than those which the prophets and Moses did say should come: That Christ should suffer, and that he should be the first that should rise from the dead, and should shew light unto the people, and to the Gentiles" (Acts 26:20-23). Paul said *none other things* than those proclaimed by Moses and the prophets for setting apart those, whom God had previously given hearing ears. His message consisted of the death and resurrection of Jesus Christ; and this, according to I Corinthians 15:1-4, is the gospel.

The seemingly difficult verse, Acts 2:38, is not a problem text if a person has the Biblical understanding of regeneration. Repentance, according to the text, precedes baptism; it is the fruit of regeneration. Since regeneration precedes repentance; and repentance precedes baptism; then, how can baptism be the cause of regeneration?

Spiritual birth, which was impossible for unregenerate Nicodemus to understand, has the common character of spiritual operations. For example, in the inspiration of the Scriptures, holy men were borne along by the Spirit to give forth the mind of God. The Spirit, therefore, breathed upon whom He pleased. Since He did not breathe upon all men alike, He discriminated. God's breathing upon holy men could not be detected by those upon whom He did not breathe. Only the effects of God's breathing could be observed. Outsiders beheld the revelation of the inspired penmen. Hence, it is the same with every person born of the Spirit. The immediate, instantaneous, and creative work of God in regeneration is unobserved by those outside of whom the Spirit works. Even the theologian of Pharisaism, Nicodemus, stood amazed at the pronouncement by Jesus Christ. "The wind bloweth where it listeth, and thou hearest the sound thereof, but canst not tell whence it cometh, and whither it goeth: so is every one that is born of the Spirit" (John 3:8).

The text, John 3:8, is one of the clearest in the New Testament on regeneration proper (adapted to the purpose of an exposition). But, before we progress too far into this exposition; we should point out that the discussion, through verse eight, is regeneration, not conversion. The subject of conversion does not begin until verse fourteen.

Some important distinctions between regeneration and conversion are:

1. Regeneration is the *immediate act of God*, in imparting the principle of life; conversion is *the act of man*, by the power of the indwelling Spirit, in repenting and believing. ". . . turn thou me, and I shall be turned; for thou art the Lord my God. Surely after that I was turned, I repented, and after that I was in-

structed . . ." (Jer. 31:18,19). ". . . helped them much which had believed through grace" (Acts 18:27). Since regeneration is presented as the act of the sovereign God, it is never presented as a duty of the sinner. The demands of the gospel, upon sinners, are limited to the terms of repentance and faith. "Testifying both to the Jews, and also to the Greeks, repentance toward God, and faith toward our Lord Jesus Christ" (Acts 20:21).

2. Regeneration is a *single act of God,* and is never repeated; conversion is the beginning of a holy life, but there are *many conversion experiences* throughout one's earthly pilgrimage. The *position* of the believer in Jesus Christ, by virtue of regeneration, can be neither increased nor decreased by anything in the recipient. (Heb. 10:10,14; Col. 2:9,11; Col. 3:1-4). *Condition* of the Christian life, however, will vary according to one's conversion experiences. (Luke 22:31-34).

3. Regeneration is *not in itself an experience;* conversion is a *series of Christian experiences.* As there is no consciousness at the time of conception in the womb, so regeneration is not a matter of consciousness to its recipient. A person knows nothing of the beginning of his existence. Conversion, however, is always an awareness of what is taking place; therefore, it is experimental. Repentance and faith are experiences known to the person born of God.

4. Regeneration is the *cause* of an individual turning to the Lord; conversion is the regenerate person *actually* turning. God does not repent and believe for man, but He enables man to do what he could not do by nature.

5. Regeneration is the Lord *opening the heart;* conversion is the person, whose heart has been opened, *turning* to Jesus Christ in faith and following the Lord in baptism (Acts 16:14,15).

6. Regeneration is a *once for all cleansing;* conversion is the *continuation of the renewal* which began in regeneration. (John 13:10; I Cor. 6:11; Titus 3:5).

7. In regeneration we have *God's power,* the power of the indwelling Spirit; in conversion the power is not *of us* but *in us* by God's sovereign choice. An understanding of this Biblical fact will remove all pride and boasting from preachers and other Christians about *their* successes.

REGENERATION IS THE CREATIVE ACT OF GOD

Regeneration must be kept within the context of redemption's application. *Application* of redemption, as well as its *planning* and *providing*, is of God. The application of redemption comprises a series of acts and processes. This is illustrated by Paul in Romans 8:28-31. "And we know that all things work together for good to them that love God, to them who are called according to his purpose. For whom he did foreknow, he also did predestinate to be conformed to the image of his Son, that he might be the first-born among many brethren. Moreover whom he did predestinate, them he also called: and whom he called, them he also justified: and whom he justified, them he also glorified. What shall we then say to these things? If God be for us, who can be against us?" Glorification, for example, cannot come first in the Divine order; it is the consummation of redemption. Order must not be violated because God is the God of order. "For because ye did it not at the first, the Lord our God made a breach upon us, for that we sought him not after the due order" (I Chron. 15:13). Regeneration is first in the order of redemption's application.

Satan is the author of confusion. Confusion, however, must exist that the approved may be made manifest. "For there must be also heresies among you, that they which are approved may be made manifest among you" (I Cor. 11:19). God has been pleased to make known a method in which His presence is brought into the souls of men. How is His presence to be brought into the souls of those chosen in Jesus Christ, that is, those for whom the Son of God died? God's initial presence is effected by being born of the Spirit. As the ordinances of God are nothing more than empty sepulchres, apart from order; so the series of acts, in redemption's application, are devoid of God's presence unless they are performed in proper sequence. Now, do you see the serious error of placing repentance, faith, baptism, and works before the beginning of life? This would be as foolish as placing a five course meal before a dead man.

The tabernacle in the wilderness illustrates that God is methodical in all His works. The Spirit of God is required to recognize the orderliness of God. When God revealed salvation to Israel, He began with Himself, where it first originated. This is the reason the ark of the covenant is the first vessel mentioned in God's directions for building the tabernacle. How could it be otherwise, and God be called the God of salvation? "Now the God of peace, that brought again from the dead our Lord Jesus, that great shepherd of the sheep, through the blood of the everlasting covenant, Make you perfect in every good work to do his will, working in you that which is well-pleasing in his sight, through Jesus Christ; to whom be glory for ever and ever. Amen." (Heb. 13:20,21). Since God was first *for* us in planning and providing; then, should He not be first *in* us in applying? The first vessel the Israelites saw was the brazen altar, but this was not the first vessel in the order given to Moses. This vessel was outside the tabernacle, but was vitally connected with the tent of meeting. The brazen altar typified the provision God made for the Israelites, to enable them to have access to the ark of the covenant which denoted His presence (Ex. 25-40).

There is blessed order in the Godhead. What the Father *decreed,* the Son *purchased,* and the Holy Spirit *applies.* The Spirit is last in the Divine order, but He is first in redemption's application. Keep in mind that the Person of Jesus Christ was not recognized by unregenerated Nicodemus. The Lord Jesus pointed him to the fact that the new birth was effected by the Spirit of God. God's Spirit would lead him to embrace Jesus Christ, and the Son of God would then reveal the Father. When this order is understood, no one will talk about Jesus Christ dying for all men and God loving all mankind.

Do not the Scriptures state that we are begotten of God? All three Persons of the Godhead are mentioned in Titus 3:5,6. "Not by the works of righteousness which we have done, but according to his mercy he saved us, by the washing of regeneration, and renewing of the Holy Ghost; which he shed on us abundantly through Jesus Christ our Saviour." Regeneration is ascribed: (1) In some places to God the Father. "Blessed be the God and Father of our Lord Jesus Christ, which according to his abundant mercy hath begotten us again unto a lively hope by the resurrection of Jesus Christ from the dead" (I Pet. 1:3). The Father's *will* is emphasized in this verse. (2) In other places the regenerated are referred to as the seed of Jesus Christ. "Yet it pleased the Lord to bruise him; he hath put him to grief: when thou shàlt make his soul an offering for sin, he shall see his seed, he shall prolong his days, and the pleasure of the Lord shall prosper in his hand"

(Is. 53:10). Here, the *merit* of the Lord Jesus should be recognized. (3) Sometimes to the Spirit of God. "The wind bloweth where it listeth, and thou hearest the sound thereof, but canst not tell whence it cometh, and whither it goeth: so is every one that is born of the Spirit" (John 3:8). In this instance the Spirit's *efficacy* is prominent.

The new creature in Christ Jesus is not produced by the cooperation of Divine and natural power. Natural man is without spiritual strength (Rom. 5:6), and the flesh is opposed to the Spirit (Gal. 5:17). Would it not be ridiculous to say that a strengthless, unholy, and passive sinner assists the omnipotent, holy, and active God in such a delicate work as creation? If Paul warns Christians about being unequally yoked together with unbelievers (II Cor. 6:14-16); then, what about the holy God and unholy man yoked together in salvation? It has been said that if creatures of several kinds should unite in unequal copulation, what would be the product but monsters? An owl's egg, though hatched by a dove, will be nothing more than a night-bird. But this is only hypothetical.

The principle of *after his kind* holds true in the spiritual as well as the physical realm. There are different kinds of flesh, and between these there is a biological difference (I Cor. 15:39). The difference is safeguarded in the nature of each kind. Man produces man; fish produces fish; animal produces animal; bird produces bird. Each flesh has its own particular sphere and function. Fish, however, does not become animal, and animal does not become man. As fish does not become animal, neither can fish cross with animal. This same principle is a fact in the spiritual sphere. "That which is born of the flesh is flesh; and that which is born of the Spirit is spirit" (John 3:6). Therefore, unsaved man does not unite with the Holy Spirit in effecting regeneration.

No Christian can believe in the Bible and the theory of evolution at the same time. The theory of evolution, which is the development of one thing into an entirely different thing by its own inherent power, is error from the pit of hell. Evolution is taught as transmutation in present day text books. Transmutation and mutation should be distinguished. Transmutation is the change from one kind to a different kind; mutation is the change which takes place within its own kind. Now, you ask, what does this have to do with the subject of regeneration? The flesh (fallen nature) of man can never become spiritual, and the Spirit can never become fallen human nature (John 3:6).

As man's essence, as man, was not altered in his fall; so God's essence, as God, was not changed in the incarnation. Man, in his upright condition, was man (Gen. 1:26; Eccl. 7:29). Changes have taken place within man, but he is still man. In the fall, man changed from an upright person to a depraved and wicked man. Regeneration does not change the chemistry of man's body; but it does apply redemption, in a creative way, to the soul. The redeemed soul awaits the redeemed body at the resurrection. God, the eternal Word, was made flesh for the purpose of redeeming fallen man. "Made flesh" does not mean that the Divine nature was made human nature, or God was changed into a man; but the Divine nature assumed a human nature without altering the Divine Person (Mal. 3:6). Hence, there are two natures, Divine and human, united in the One Person, the Lord Jesus Christ. There have been changes in God's methods of operation, but never a change in His Divine Person or His eternal purpose.

Theistic evolution is the theory held by many unbelieving theologians. They are fearful of being classified as unscientific, so they have adopted evolution as God's method of creation. These same theologians, for the most part, view the first eleven chapters of Genesis as allegorical or mythological. Theistic evolution starts man as far down the scale of minute things as possible, and through the process of evolution man becomes civilized and educated to the extent that he becomes like God. If God used evolution as a means of creation, He would have created man imperfect and depraved. But the truth is, God created man upright (finite perfection). "Lo, this only have I found, that God hath made man upright; but they have sought out many inventions" (Eccl. 7:29). The complete story of man can be stated in three words: creation, degeneration, and regeneration. Man, therefore, had no place until he became the subject of creative power. This is true both physically and spiritually. The testimony of the Psalmist was, "Know ye that the Lord he is God: it is he that made us, and not we ourselves . . ." (Ps. 100:3). Thus, as man contributed nothing to his physical creation; neither does he give assistance to his spiritual birth.

Those who believe that man, in his depraved condition, must make the first move to become a new creature are as heretical as those who embrace theistic evolution. This makes a blind, deaf, and helpless sinner arise to the place of letting the omnipotent, omniscient, omnipresent, and sovereign God make him a new creature.

Regeneration is not a product of the depraved human will, plus the work of the Holy Spirit. It is the creative act of God, sovereignly wrought, in a heart that is depraved and unwilling by nature. The new birth makes the unwilling, willing; and the whosoever won't becomes the whosoever will. Our Lord taught, within the context of our subject, that ". . . everyone that doeth evil hateth the light, neither cometh to the light, lest his deeds should be reproved (discovered)" (John 3:20). Again, He said to the Pharisees, ". . . ye will not come to me that ye might have life" (John 5:40). Depraved man hates the One true and living God (Rom. 1:30), the light of Divine truth (John 3:20), and those who are united to the God of the Bible and embrace His truth (John 15:18). This hatred for God and truth, and unwillingness to come to the true and living God is changed only by the power of grace in regeneration.

Did not Nicodemus come to Jesus Christ in his unregenerate condition? Yes, but his coming was in the sense that most religionists go to church and Sunday School. Not all depraved people live in the gutter of sin. Many of them enjoy assembling, for what they call church related activities. Their *god* is one whom they have conceived in their depraved minds. They do not fear or hate *their god*. But as soon as the sovereign and holy God of the Bible is proclaimed, their hatred is manifested; and they desire to kill IIim and all who stand up for Him (Luke 4:25-32; John 8:33-47).

Pure Bible preaching is very discriminating. You can tell Cain from Abel when *sacrifice* is the subject; Jacob from Esau when *love* is the topic; and Daniel from Nebuchadnezzar when *sovereignty* is the thought for investigation.

The sacrifice of Jesus Christ discriminates between the gospel of redemption and the social gospel. When the vicariousness of Christ's death is preached, everything in natural man is condemned. His self-love, self-righteousness, and self-justification are discovered and condemned. This is something the unregenerate man despises; it does something to his unbelieving ego, and he begins to rebel. Paul instructs us about this very thing in Galatians 4:28,29. "Now we, brethren, as Isaac was, are the children

of promise. But as then he that was born after the flesh persecuted him that was born after the Spirit, even so it is now." We
are told that, during the reformation, as the truth of justification
through faith began to spread throughout the European countries,
bitter persecution broke out with a deadly cry. The cry went forth,
"Put these people to death who believe in salvation through grace,
who do not believe that they can be saved by penances and human
merit; do everything possible to rid the world of them." As it
was in the depraved human heart then, even so it is now. The
difference between then and now is not in the deceitful and wicked
heart, but in the restraint of civil authority. Let the Christian
be thankful for such restraint in God's providential dealings
with him.

As there was a division in Christ's day over the subjects of His
death and resurrection, so it is impossible to insist upon the spiritual teaching respecting these matters without causing division.
"I am the good shepherd, and know my sheep, and am known
of mine. As the Father knoweth me, even so know I the Father:
and I lay down my life for the sheep. And other sheep I have,
which are not of this fold; them also I must bring, and they shall
hear my voice: and there shall be one fold, and one shepherd.
Therefore doth my Father love me, because I lay down my life,
that I might take it again. No man taketh it from me, but I lay
it down of myself. I have power to lay it down, and I have power
to take it again. This commandment have I received of my Father.
There was a division therefore again among the Jews for these
sayings" (John 10:14-19). Advocates of the social gospel are not
concerned about the cause of social evils. They spend their energies
treating symptoms. They, like Cain, have gone the way of human
merit and works. These modernists have a hatred, as intense as
Cain had for Abel, toward those who promote the truth of *free
grace*. Jude said, "Woe unto them! for they have gone in the way
of Cain . . ." (Jude 11). These false teachers believe that the
preachers of free grace are enemies to their program of social
reform.

Our Lord came not to socially reform society, but to redeem
the elect. A clear Biblical view of this fact is set forth in Luke
12:13,14. "And one of the company said unto him, Master, speak
to my brother, that he divide the inheritance with me. And he
said unto him, Man, who made me a judge or a divider over you?"

At first glance, Christ's refusal to interfere between these two brothers seems astonishing. Is there not a question of justice to be decided? And who is so competent to deal with it as the eternal Son of God? Why does Jesus Christ refuse to enter into the dispute? There are two ways of dealing with men: (1) Regeneration—internal change by the work of the Holy Spirit; and (2) Reformation—external change by formulating laws, thus seeking to change moral, social, and political evils. Our Lord refused to interfere because His mission was not to socialize, but to redeem the elect of God.

It is imperative, at this point, that we emphasize the office and work of Jesus Christ. The Son of God came to give His life a ransom for many, and to proclaim and establish principles.

1. The Lord Jesus disclaimed His position of Judge or Divider at His first coming. "For God sent not his Son into the world to condemn the world; but that the world through him might be saved" (John 3:17). He reminded the person who spoke that he, as well as his brother, was moved by covetousness. A person may be as selfish in seeking his rights as another man is in withholding them from him. There is a manifestation of this on every hand today.

2. Our Lord forbids oppression. Christ did not take from the oppressor and give to the oppressed, neither did He encourage the oppressed to take from the oppressor. He did not exercise this prerogative at His first coming.

3. The purpose of Christ at His first coming was not to found His Body on outward law and jurisprudence, but on a spiritual disposition applied by the Spirit in regeneration. The gospel, however, does not interfere with civil rights and human laws (Rom. 13) ; but human government cannot legislate righteousness. Covetousness often presents itself as prudence; the only corrective is the grace of God. Provision for temporal need is not the ruling principle of life. Wealth is not necessary to an ideal life. "For ye know the grace of our Lord Jesus Christ, that, though he was rich, yet for your sakes he became poor, that ye through his poverty might be rich" (II Cor. 8:9).

What is the role of the church in this world? The church does not need the coercive arm of the state to accomplish God's will in the world. If that were required, the power of the Spirit in regeneration would be inadequate. God instituted civil authority as a moral governor of the world to extend to all citizens without exception. While it is clear that human government is Divinely instituted for all mankind, it is equally revealed that the church is not to be controlled by the state. The realm of civil affairs is outside of the church. The church's jurisdiction extends only to her own members, and the jurisdiction of the state extends only to its own citizens.

The redemptive work of Jesus Christ discriminates between all the Abels and Cains today. Are you an Abel by the application of Christ's blood in regeneration? Now, for the second question; are you a Cain because of your love for the social gospel, which rejects and despises the sacrifice of Christ?

The particular love of God distinguishes between *free grace* and *free will*. Esau and Jacob offer a much stronger case for the freeness of God's grace than Ishmael and Isaac. It can no longer be debated that the reason Ishmael was not chosen was because he was the son of Hagar, the bondwoman. Paul shows that the same mother bore both Esau and Jacob by the same father. And before they were born, God declared that the elder should serve the younger. This was contrary to Hebrew custom.

Those who oppose free grace present the case of Esau and Jacob in a national sense. They say it refers not to individuals, but only to the national life of Israel. Thus, they compare this passage to Malachi 1:1-5. But what they forget is, the words of Malachi are only an explanation of the spiritual condition of Esau and Jacob. Malachi was talking about the spiritual, not the temporal, condition of Israel. His prophecy came long after Esau and Jacob were dead, yet the Lord directed the murmuring Jews to His regard for Esau and Jacob *personally*. It cannot be denied that the persons of Esau and Jacob were personally in the mind of the Lord as He directed Malachi to give warning to their descendants. *God's everlasting love is the cause of His choice of particular persons to salvation.*

We hear so much today about God's elected plan. Let us investigate the word *plan*. Plan means a method of action or procedure; a project or definite purpose. No student of Scripture denies that God has a purpose, and that His purpose is definite (Eph. 3:11; Is. 46:10,11; Rom. 8:28-30; II Tim. 1:9). The questions that must be answered are: (1) Did God plan (purpose) to save all mankind? If He planned to save all, then why are not all saved? (2) Did God plan (purpose) to save some, that is believers? Since He saves only believers, then He did not purpose to save all.

Love is, in its very nature, particular and personal. "The Lord hath appeared of old unto me, saying, Yea, I have loved thee with an everlasting love: therefore with loving-kindness have I drawn thee" (Jer. 31:3). God's love is not an inclination of His nature; it is an act of His will. There is no imperfection in God's love; He is all-sufficient. Divine love for all, which, if not perfected in all would be incomplete. But the great theme of Romans eight is the love of the sovereign God manifested toward the elect. The love is all from God's side, and we can account for it only as we are in Christ Jesus, Whom to know is life eternal. Thus, God's love shall be perfected in all for whom it was intended. It has been said that sovereignty holds the scale of love; justice holds the other scale.

The Esaus quickly manifest their natural reasoning. They always argue from reprobation, by presenting it as something awful from God's standpoint. The truth of reprobation excites all unenlightened and prejudiced minds. Hence, their erroneous conclusion is that God is unjust in giving some mercy and others justice. But who can find any injustice in that? There is no such thing as sovereign, unmerited, damnation. God ordains none but sinners to punishment. He does not force any into sin against their wills; He just leaves them to their own natural desires. Men are not lost because they are hardened, but they are hardened because they are lost. Finally, no person is damned who wants to be saved. If one does not want to be saved, then why be angry with God because he is not chosen? *Giving* and *receiving* are relative terms.

All the Jacobs reason from the sovereignty of God. They believe that God can do what He pleases with His own, but how humbled they are for God's unmerited favor extended toward them. "For we ourselves also were sometimes foolish, disobedient, deceived, serving divers lusts and pleasures, living in malice and envy, hateful, and hating one another. But after that the kindness and love of God our Saviour toward man appeared, Not by works of righteousness which we have done, but according to his mercy he saved us, by the washing of regeneration and renewing of the Holy Ghost; Which he shed on us abundantly through Jesus Christ our

Saviour; That being justified by his grace, we should be made heirs according to the hope of eternal life" (Titus 3:3-7).

God's absolute sovereignty discriminates between the Daniels and Nebuchadnezzars. King Nebuchadnezzar was troubled in spirit because of some dreams he had dreamed. He called for the wise men of Babylon to interpret them, but they were incapable; so Daniel was summoned to explain the meaning of the dreams. The secret was revealed to Daniel (Dan. 2:19-23). The interpretation was beyond human ingenuity. Later the king had a tree vision; and, once again, Daniel was invited to give the interpretation (Dan. 4:20-27). But, in the face of this interpretation, the king claimed honor belonging to God alone (Dan. 4:30,31). God showed Nebuchadnezzar that He is sovereign; even so, our God shall manifest His absolute sovereignty to the world in the future.

God's sovereignty is the first of all rights, the foundation of all righteousness, and the ground of all justice. If God is not God, Who is He? God is not the object of judgment by any creature, but He alone judges all creatures. God is as sovereign in redemption's application as He was in its provision.

THE HOLY SPIRIT IS THE AGENT OF REGENERATION

Nicodemus had objected to the new birth because he did not understand how it could be accomplished. Christ's term, new birth, had a peculiar significance to a Jew. Were not all his privileges secured to him by birth? Did he not boast of the fact that Abraham was his father? Thus, such terms as *born again, begotten of God,* and *born of God* were appropriate for those who were of the seed of Abraham. Our Lord was showing Nicodemus that just as natural birth ushers one into conscious existence on an earthly plane, so a spiritual birth is required to usher the same person into conscious life on a heavenly plane.

There are other figures of the new birth employed in the Scriptures, and they are equally significant. Paul, the apostle to the Gentiles, used such terms as *quickened* (Eph. 2:1), *creation* (II Cor. 5:17), *workmanship* (Eph. 2:10), and *regeneration* (Titus 3:5). Gentiles were more familiar with artistic and mechanical operations; therefore, the Holy Spirit chose these designations for them.

The word *regeneration* is found only twice in the New Testament. It is applied not only to human beings (Titus 3:5), but also to the renewed heaven and earth of the coming kingdom (Matt. 19:28). Only in Titus 3:5 is the word used in the sense of applied redemption. Regeneration and the new birth do not represent successive stages in the work of redemption's application; they refer to the same work of the sovereign Spirit.

Christ taught Nicodemus that the Agent of regeneration is the Holy Spirit. He used the wind as a symbol of the work of the Spirit in accomplishing the work of regeneration. "The wind bloweth where it listeth, and thou hearest the sound thereof, but canst not tell whence it cometh, and whither it goeth; so is every one that is born of the Spirit" (John 3:8). The three divisions of this verse are: (1) *A physical fact*—"The wind bloweth where it listeth;" (2) *The operation* of the Spirit—under the emblem of the wind with its various characteristics; and (3) *The result* of the operation of the Spirit—is regeneration. Thus, the three portions of this verse hinge on three words: *wind, Spirit, and birth.* "He that observeth the wind shall not sow; and he that regardeth the clouds shall not reap. As thou knowest not what is the way of the spirit, nor how the bones do grow in the womb of her that is with child: even so thou knowest not the works of God who maketh all. In the morning sow thy seed, and in the evening withhold not thine hand: for thou knowest not whether shall prosper, either this or that, or whether they both shall be alike good" (Eccl. 11:4-6).

The *physical fact* presents the wind as blowing where it pleases, as it pleases, when it pleases, in the manner it pleases, and on whom it pleases. Its unaccountable changes are the result of material laws as fixed and stable as that by which the planets revolve. Science has made only slight progress in seeking to trace the laws of the wind. The reason is because of man's limited understanding of natural laws. To men, the actions of the wind may seem to be inconsistent; but in reality, there is Divine order. Human research cannot discover any law by which this seeming inequality, in the movement of the wind, is ordered.

Some of the greatest powers in nature are invisible. For instance, when a tornado hits an area with destructive force, the results only, not the wind, are seen. When a giant magnet is seen drawing iron, one does not see the strange influence by which the attraction is effected. The law of gravitation is something known to everyone with ordinary intelligence, yet the keenest eyes have never seen gravitation.

There is something mysterious about the wind. Man does not know where it comes from or where it is going. But he knows that the wind exists because he hears its sound and sees its fructifying effects. "Awake, O north wind; and come, thou south; blow upon my garden, that the spices thereof may flow out. Let my beloved come into his garden, and eat his pleasant fruits" (Song of Sol. 4:16). When we see the leaves of a forest move to and fro, we know the wind is there; but where it came from and where it is going are unknown to us. Thus, there is both a mystery and a manifestation. Man cannot penetrate the mystery of its origin, neither the final effects of its work.

Christ borrows a comparison from the order of nature. The fact that the wind blows cannot be denied. Hearing the wind is evidence of the fact. And since man knows neither its beginning nor ending, it is a mystery.

The following are characteristics of the wind:

1. It is not accountable to man. The wind does not act according to man's beckoning. It flows through the world freely; not moving at the command of one man, neither caring for the prohibition of another. Hence, it is answerable to no creature.

2. It is irresistible in its work. It blesses some and destroys others. The same wind that brings refreshing rain to one place drives the clouds away and causes drought in another area (Ps. 147:18; Prov. 25:23).

3. It is incapable of being comprehended. There are some things about the wind which defy all effort of human comprehension. Though these things cannot be comprehended, they are apprehended because the evidence of its existence is clearly seen.

4. It is imperceptible to the eye. The wind is one of the few things in nature that is invisible. We can see the rain and the snow, but not the wind. "The heavens declare the glory of God; and the firmament sheweth his handiwork" (Ps. 19:1). "Because that which may be known of God is manifest in them; for God hath shewed it unto them. For the invisible things of him from the creation of the world are clearly seen, being understood by the things that are made, even his eternal power and Godhead; so that they are without excuse" (Rom. 1:19,20).

5. It is absolutely essential to man's existence. If a dead calm were to continue, all living things would die (Rev. 7:1-3). The atmosphere is an envelopment of air that enwraps our globe, and gets lighter and thinner until it gradually disappears from forty to fifty miles from the earth's surface. It is the only element in which man can live. As still water stagnates, so will still air. The benevolent Creator, in His providential dealings with mankind, is careful that the wind never remains perfectly still.

6. It has life-giving properties. This is revealed in the advice given by physicians for better health.

7. It works without and with means. It works without means in the tornado and with means of water in the hurricane.

The wind is an emblem of the Holy Spirit. The influences of the Spirit are *vital, sovereign,* and *mysterious.* ". . . And the Spirit of God moved upon the face of the waters" (Gen. 1:2). "And the Lord God formed man of the dust of the ground, and breathed into his nostrils the breath of life; and man became a living soul"

(Gen. 2:7). "Thou sendest forth thy spirit, they are created . . ." (Ps. 104:30). ". . . the skin covered them above: but there was no breath in them. Then said he unto me, Prophesy unto the wind, prophesy, son of man, and say to the wind, Thus said the Lord God; Come from the four winds, O breath, and breathe upon these slain, that they may live . . . and the breath came into them, and they lived . . ." (Ezek. 37:8-10).

There is a double signification of the Greek word for Spirit; the word means both *spirit* and *breathe.* Thus, we may read either "the wind bloweth," or "the Spirit breathes."

These are some characteristics of the Holy Spirit in regeneration:

1. The free action of the Spirit is vividly portrayed in the Scriptures. He does as He wills, but He wills the eternal purpose of the Godhead. The third Person of the Godhead is the Spirit of the Father and of the Son. His purpose is to regenerate those whom the Father elected and the Son purchased.

   God alone has free will in the absolute sense. The Spirit's arbitrariness, which characterizes His work, is not the same as arbitrariness in man. Arbitrariness in man is revealed when he refuses any norm or standard above himself. Human arbitrariness, therefore, is always without a standard; but God cannot be guilty of arbitrariness because He is His own law. There is no standard above Himself. It is impossible to subject God to a law above Himself that would restrict His own actions. God's sovereignty rules out arbitrariness because His sovereignty forms the enduring foundation of all authority. Man must not reason by starting from a law above God, for there is no law above God. He must begin with God, Who is above arbitrariness. Is the hand of God ever shortened that it cannot save those whom He purposed to save?

2. The Spirit is irresistible in regeneration. Opposition to the Spirit and resistence thereof by men, pertains only to the external dispensation of grace. Acts 7:51 does not refer to the subjective work of the Spirit in regeneration, but to the objective proclamation of the gospel: "Ye stiffnecked and uncircumcised in heart and ears, ye do always resist the Holy Ghost: as your fathers did, so do ye." When you contrast this verse with John 3:8 and Romans 9:19, the meaning is clear. The resistance by

these Jews was not to the Spirit of God within them, for they were destitute of the Spirit. They resisted the Spirit of God in His ministers, and particularly in Stephen. Their subjective darkness resisted the objective light of the gospel. This fact is illustrated in John 1:5, "And the light shineth in darkness; and the darkness comprehended it not."

The Holy Spirit cannot be resisted in regeneration because He works immediately upon the subconsciousness of man. As the child knows nothing of the genesis of his own existence, so the Christian knows nothing of the beginning of his spiritual existence.

3. The Spirit's work in regeneration is incomprehensible. God's mysterious dealings with the souls of men are never without reason, but the reason is known only to Himself.

As there is both a mystery and a manifestation in the incarnation, so there is also mystery and manifestation in regeneration. "And without controversy great is the mystery of godliness: God was manifest in the flesh, justified in the Spirit, seen of angels, preached unto the Gentiles, believed on in the world, received up into glory" (I Tim. 3:16). "To whom God would make known what is the riches of the glory of this mystery among the Gentiles; which is Christ in you, the hope of glory" (Col. 1:27).

The word *mystery* signifies something hidden. Even though the incarnation has been manifested, yet it is still a mystery because it can never be fully comprehended. Grace is manifested in regeneration, but the new birth itself remains a mystery. That we live we know, but how we live we cannot describe. Thus, the mighty gale, which blows from heaven, wafts its way into the souls of the elect performing a work that is manifested only by conversion and sanctification. God has not chosen to reveal everything to men; therefore, He said through Moses, "The secret things belong unto the Lord our God: but those things which are revealed belong unto us and to our children for ever, that we may do all the words of this law" (Deut. 29:29).

4. The Spirit's work in the new birth is invisible. The first movement of the Spirit in redemption's application is unseen. It is the secret, creative, and immediate work of God in the soul;

therefore, not subject to the consciousness of man. Though the impartation of life in the soul of the elect be momentous, yet it is one of which man has no immediate evidence.

Man is so accustomed to associate great events in history with outward display, it is difficult for him to be divested of the idea that external significance is inseparable from real importance. In the spiritual realm, things of real and lasting importance do not appear before men with great display of outward show. The conception, birth, and early life of our Lord is a manifestation of this Biblical fact. Thus, it is with every person born of the Spirit. The mysterious agent of the Holy Spirit, in the work of regeneration, is unseen by man.

5. The third Person of the Godhead is absolutely essential for man's survival on earth. There is no place where God is not. As God is not measured by time, so He cannot be limited by space. As no place can be without God, so no place can compass and contain Him. "Whither shall I go from thy spirit? or whither shall I flee from thy presence? If I ascend up into heaven, thou art there: if I make my bed in hell, behold, thou are there" (Ps. 139:7,8). "Can any hide himself in secret places that I shall not see him? saith the Lord . . ." (Jer. 23:24). Every man is dependent on God for his existence. "For in him we live, and move, and have our being . . ." (Acts 17:28). The natural life which men live is from God. The beginning, maintaining, and continuing of life are all dependent on the power and providence of God.

6. The Holy Spirit has life-giving properties. Regeneration is the communication of life by the operation of the Spirit. This act of the Spirit in the soul makes man a fit subject for the effectual call and conversion. Life and death are absolute opposites, and any thought of a third state between them must be abandoned. The state of hovering between life and death is unthinkable. The immediate agency of the Holy Spirit is the efficient cause of regeneration. "And you hath he quickened, who were dead in trespasses and sins" (Eph. 2:1). "For God, who commanded the light to shine out of darkness, hath shined in our hearts, to give the light of the knowledge of the glory of God in the face of Jesus Christ" (II Cor. 4:6).

7. The Spirit of God works without means in regeneration, and

with means in conversion. Preparatory grace must not be interpreted as a means to prepare sinners for the impartation of life. Nothing prepares for such quickening. Life comes not from anything in men, but entirely from the work of God. All preparatory grace, as some call it, accomplishes is that God by providence disposes life and arranges its course until the time of regeneration. The time of regeneration is called, in Ezekiel 16:8, "the time of love." As the child, in Ezekiel 16, was preserved until the time God spoke life into its soul, so the person whom God gave to Christ will be preserved physically until the day of regeneration. Preparatory grace contributes nothing to the origin of life, which comes by the immediate work of the Spirit. As the origin of seed must be distinguished from the cultivation of a field, so the origin of life in regeneration must be distinguished from conversion experiences in the life of believers. The Spirit working with means in conversion will be the subject of John 3:14-18.

God's act of giving life to the spiritually dead is distinct from His truth, just as the faculty of sight is distinct from light. Since quickening is an immediate and creative act, no instrumental and secondary causes are connected with it. The Scripture is effective only in those who are renewed (I Cor. 2:12-14) ; it cannot produce life. Man sees because he is born of the Spirit (John 3:3). Once the faculty of sight is given, the recipient is guided by the word which is indispensable to conversion.

Does the act of regeneration precede, accompany, or follow the hearing of the gospel? In order to answer this question correctly, one must consider what is meant by the word *hearing*. Is this an *ear that hears*, or the organ of the human body, called *ear?* To be technical, the Holy Spirit may perform His work of regeneration before, during, or after the *external call* of the gospel. But, one thing for sure, if man is to hear the effectual call of God, there must first be a work of God in his soul.

Scripture distinguishes the influence of the Holy Spirit from that of the word of God, and declares that such an influence is necessary for proper reception of the truth (John 6:64,65; I Cor. 2:12-15; Eph. 1:17,20). Notice particularly the example of Lydia. "(She) heard us (singular), whose heart the Lord opened (single act) that she attended (result or purpose) unto the things which were spoken by Paul" (Acts 16:14).

God's election and Christ's blood, the two great causes of salvation, cannot save man apart from the application of redemption by the Holy Spirit. Thus, the application of redemption is of God (I Cor. 1:30). Never was a sick person healed by a prepared, but unapplied medicine (Heb. 1:1-3). Adam's disobedience harms all who are in him; Christ's blood profits only those who are in Him by regeneration. When Christ died the ransom was paid (Matt. 20:28; Mark 10:45). However, the elect continue in sin because of depravity until, by the work of the Holy Spirit, the new birth is actually applied in them.

UNION WITH GOD IS THE RESULT OF REGENERATION

The effect of the Spirit's work in regeneration is union with God. Union with Christ is a great and impenetrable mystery; it should be defined in order to keep us from falling into serious error. When and how does this union take place? To say it occurs at the point of faith is not the whole truth. There are five stages of this union:

1. This union was planned in God's eternal decree with His Son. Thus, a relation was established between the Father and those given to Christ in the covenant of redemption. All subsequent relations spring from this eternal covenant (Heb. 13:20,21).

2. The provision of this union was initiated when Christ, in the incarnation, passed from purpose into actual existence. Christ, in the flesh, carried all whom the Father gave Him in the loins of His grace. As Adam carried all the children of men in the loins of his flesh; so Scriptures teach that when Jesus Christ died and rose, we died and rose with and in Him.

3. The union is actually effected when the elect are regenerated. Union actually takes place when, in the time of love, the Spirit implants the principle of life in the souls of those for whom Christ died. Until regeneration, the mystic union was hidden in the eternal purpose of God.

4. The consciousness of the union of the regenerated comes through the exercise of faith. Consciousness of this union must be distinguished from regeneration. The faculty of faith, which was implanted in regeneration, may not immediately manifest itself in conscious faith and conversion. For example, a child possesses its mother from the first moment of his existence; but a conscious enjoyment of this possession is awakened and increased after birth. Therefore, the conscious enjoyment of our union with Christ is awakened and increased after the new birth. Even though we are some time coming to a conscious understanding of our union with Christ, the subjective union itself existed from the time of regeneration.

5. The last stage of union does not attain its fullest unveiling until believers see Jesus Christ face to face (I John 3:2,3).

Union of Christ and His people has a nature peculiar to itself;

it may be compared to other unions, but it can never be fully explained by them. Who can explain the bond between body and soul, mother and child, vine and branches, and man and wife? Therefore, realization of mystical union drives the elect from themselves to God for an answer to the mystery. The answer is made known only by the indwelling Spirit. "For ye have not received the spirit of bondage again to fear; but ye have received the Spirit of adoption, whereby we cry, Abba, Father. The Spirit itself (Himself) beareth witness with our spirit, that we are the children of God: And if children, then heirs; heirs of God, and joint-heirs with Christ; if so be that we suffer with him, that we may be also glorified together" (Rom. 8:15-17).

As believers cannot understand the hypostatical union of the two natures in Christ's Person, so we cannot comprehend the mystical union of Christ and believers. The souls of the redeemed, however, are satisfied to find these mysteries expounded in the word of God. Men are not at liberty to interpret this mystical union according to their own opinions. Finite men are not expected to be able to comprehend the infinite; but what they are unable to comprehend, they apprehend by faith.

Beware of a very subtle teaching concerning the subject of union with Christ! That erroneous teaching begins from the antithesis (contrast) existing between God and man: "God is the creator, man is the creature; God is infinite, man is finite; God dwells in the eternal, man lives in the temporal; God is holy, man is unholy." There is nothing wrong with this antithesis, but let us proceed to the next statement: "In the first place, there is God; this is the thesis (proposition). Opposed to this thesis in God, the antithesis (contrast) appears in men. Thus, the thesis and antithesis find their reconciliation (synthesis) in the Mediator, who is both infinite and finite." Now, let us observe the subtlety of the heresy: "Christ is Mediator equally between Jews and Gentiles, God and man, spirit and body, heaven and hell, and time and eternity." And, finally, the climax of this false teaching is damnable: "The reconciliation causes all contrasts to disappear." The contrast between God and man, heaven and hell, shall never disappear. A reconciliation must be brought about for the sinner; but this reconciliation does not destroy the contrast between God and man, neither between heaven and hell.

Nature's best illustration concerning the manner of regeneration, is the art of grafting. Grafting has always been a wonder to men. The trunk, into which the good branch is grafted, is absolutely wild. By nature, the wild trunk sucks the sap and forces it throughout the tree. But the graft has the wonderful power of converting the sap and vital forces, of the wild trunk, into something good; thus, causing the tree to bear good fruit. This does not mean that the good branch has no opposition from the old trunk. The wild trunk vigorously resists the good branch by forming wild shoots below the graft. In this manner, the old trunk seeks to prevent the sap from flowing through the good branch to the bud. Therefore, the wild shoots below the graft must be cut off.

Depraved man, by nature, is compared with Ishmael. Ishmael, a wild ass, was sinful by nature. All his works were motivated by the energy of his wicked and deceitful heart (Jer. 17:9). Ishmael, the man after the flesh, could never become Isaac. Isaac, the son of promise, represents the work of regeneration. As Ishmael represents man born of the flesh, so Isaac typifies man born of the Spirit.

Nicodemus, the unregenerate ruler of the Jews, is compared with Ishmael. As Ishmael had observed the ordinances, so Nicodemus was one who followed the vain traditions of his fathers (I Pet. 1:18). But the natural seed of the Jews, with whom the teacher of Israel was affiliated, could not produce spiritual life. By nature, Nicodemus could not produce the new birth, any more than the wild trunk of a tree could produce good fruit. Thus, as Isaac came in solely by the promise and power of God, so Nicodemus must be born of the Spirit.

The regenerated man is one man with two natures. Scripture represents the Christian as a new creature (II Cor. 5:17). His body is the same, but the disposition of the soul is changed. The unrighteous soul of man, by nature, is made righteous by the uncreated righteousness of God. Regeneration brings in a new nature which contends with and conquers the corrupt nature. Isaac, born into the tent where only Ishmael had formerly dwelt, is an illustration of the new birth. Isaac (the new nature) must contend with Ishmael (the old nature) until the tent (the body) falls in death and Ishmael (the flesh) is cast out. A husbandman does not cut down an engrafted tree, but only takes away wild branches below the graft; neither does a regenerated man crucify (mutilate) his body, but mortifies the deeds thereof.

Is regeneration the act of making man a partaker of the Divine nature? "Whereby are given unto us exceeding great and precious promises: that by these ye might be partakers of the divine nature, having escaped the corruption that is in the world through lust" (II Pet. 1:4). "Made partaker of the divine nature" is an important but confusing phrase to many. This cannot be understood in a literal sense, for man can never be a partaker of the Divine essence. The word *Divine* means Godlike, and *partaker* means companion. Thus, the word *nature* cannot be essence or substance; it is disposition or moral qualities. The apostle was teaching that, when we put off the vices of the flesh, we shall be partakers of the blessing of God in a way proper to believers. We shall be one with God so far as our capacity allows. Peter contrasted heavenly glory to the corruption of the world. The moment the new life tastes the graciousness of the Lord, the Christian is spoiled for the world. The Lord's desire for His people is that we be more and more conformed to His image, even now. The reference, therefore, is not to a God nature; but a Godlike nature. The Godlike nature refers to those Divine qualities, called in other passages of Scripture, *image of God* (Col. 1:15), and *life of God* (John 10:10). As God became like us to redeem, so we become like Him in regeneration.

Jesus Christ is the Son of God, and Christians are the children of God; but this does not make either the Sonship of Christ or the sonship of Christians the same nature. Christ is the Son by eternal generation; believers are sons of God by regeneration. Hence, *to be the Son forever,* and *to be adopted as a son* are contrasts. Another contrast is, Christ has the Divine nature inherently in Himself; believers are only partakers of the Divine nature.

Life is communicated immediately by regeneration, but once life is imparted the promises become a living message to the new life. The mere words of a promise will not communicate Divine life to men's souls. Sanctification, rather than union with Christ, is emphasized in the first part of II Peter 1. The "exceeding great and precious promises" are given to those who have obtained "like precious faith" (II Pet. 1:1). God calls His people to pursue glory as their object, thus gaining victory over their enemies. Since those united with Christ have escaped corruption of the world, Peter exhorts them to flee inward corruption, and add to their faith Christian graces. Like precious faith will produce like precious practice.

Regeneration signifies a new birth. God first makes man new by giving him a new heart (Ezek. 36:26). The new commandment itself is not new, but it is new to the regenerated man because he possesses a new understanding (I John 2:7). New life, which is the fruit of regeneration, must be cultivated and grow before it becomes a mighty tree of righteousness (Ps. 1:1-3). Years may pass before the stature of manhood is reached. Even though the Christian possesses a new heart, life, standing, commandment, and state; there are many glorious new things awaiting him in the future. They are a new body, name, robe, song, and home.

REGENERATION IS THE IMPARTATION OF THE PRINCIPLE OF SPIRITUAL LIFE

Regeneration involves: (1) *A new relation to God.* The Father is the fountain of grace. Grace is the free and unmerited love of God arising from His own sovereign will. "Who hath saved us, and called us with an holy calling, not according to our works, but according to his own purpose and grace . . ." (II Tim. 1:9). This is to the praise of the Father's glory. "To the praise of the glory of his grace, wherein he hath made us accepted in the beloved" (Eph. 1:6). This grace manifestly appears in the election of men to the position of sons. It was not necessary that the Father have sons, since He had always had a dear and beloved Son. He was always well pleased with the eternal Son; therefore, it was an act of grace for God the Father to take out sons from among mankind, by redemption and regeneration, into His family. (2) *A new dynamic,* which flows from union with Jesus Christ. This union was effected by regeneration. The application of Christ's redemption to the soul is to the praise of Christ's glory. "That we should be to the praise of his glory, who first trusted in Christ" (Eph. 1:12). (3) *A new direction of will,* which is the fruit of the indwelling Holy Spirit. Man's will before regeneration is directed against God, but after the new birth it is subject to the guidance of the Holy Spirit. God liberates the enslaved will of fallen man in regeneration. Thus, the new man is led, by the indwelling Spirit, not dragged or forced. This is to the praise of the Spirit's glory. "In whom ye also trusted, after that ye heard the word of truth, the gospel of your salvation: in whom also after that ye believed, ye were sealed with that Holy Spirit of promise, Which is the earnest of our inheritance until the redemption of the purchased possession, unto the praise of his glory" (Eph. 1:13,14). The *word of truth* can be heard only after the application of redemption, which changes the direction of the will to embrace the message of the gospel.

The new birth is not the removal of anything from the sinner, neither the changing of anything within the depraved person; it is the impartation of the principle of spiritual life to the elect. This principle of life never existed before in the chosen. Thus, he possesses a new heart, a new spirit, and a new ego (a conscious element that knows spiritual experience). Every descendant of

Adam is born with an ego turned away from God; but, in the new birth, he is given an ego that embraces the Lord Jesus as Saviour and Lord.

There is much controversy concerning redemption's application. Some earnestly contend that regeneration, calling, conversion, and justification all occur at the same instant. Hence, they say that much confusion has arisen over conceiving these as occurring in chronological order. Their reasoning is that sensation and perception are not separated in time, even though the former is the cause of the latter. Their concluding argument states that the theory of regeneration, which makes man purely passive, has a benumbing effect upon preaching. They say, this antinomian dependence on the Spirit extracts all vitality from the pulpit and all sense of responsibility from the hearer. They strongly oppose the view that regeneration is so entirely due to God that in no part of it is man active.

A classic example of the misunderstanding of redemption's application is seen in the footnotes of the Scofield Reference Bible, page 1117. The four points he emphasizes are:

1. The necessity of the new birth grows out of the incapacity of the natural man to *see and enter.*
2. The new birth is not a reformation of the old nature, but a creative act of the Holy Spirit.
3. The condition of the new birth is faith in Christ crucified.
4. Through the new birth the believer becomes a partaker of the Divine nature.

The first two points on regeneration by Scofield are scriptural; but the last two demonstrate a lack of Biblical understanding and interpretation. Since when have God's creative acts been conditional? Upon what were the creative acts of Genesis I, conditioned? Was it necessary that God get the approval of a nonentity before He could create an entity? It seems that many people have lost sight of the fact that the new birth is the creative act of God in the soul of a man who lacks faith to embrace the gospel. No instrumental or secondary causes are connected with God's creative act.

When man's faith is made the condition of the new birth, then necessity is laid upon God to regenerate that person. This is too ridiculous to even think, much less for anyone to propagate. I shall begin to expose this heresy by asking a question. Did God, when He created the world, act because of any outside pressure? The answer is simple. There was nothing outside to bring any pressure. God, therefore, chose to create, not for the sake of the creation; but for His own pleasure and glory. The same principle is applied to all God's creative acts, whether to the heavens and earth, man, or the new creature in Christ Jesus.

God did not create for the sake of His creatures, neither does He redeem men for their own sake. There were no creatures in fact when He created; and creatures in view must exist for their Creator, not the Creator for the creatures. As there were no creatures in fact when God created, so there were no human beings in fact when God chose them in Christ before the foundation of the world. The elect persons in view, therefore, must exist for the sovereign God, Who elected them. God does not exist for persons who decide (?) they would like to have Him as their Saviour.

Three important questions must be raised and answered before redemption and its application can be properly understood: (1) Did God plan for Himself or His creatures? (2) Did God create for Himself or His creatures? (3) Does God live for Himself or His creatures?

Creation is the manifestation of the work of an intelligent Being, the One Who planned or purposed, and works all things according to His plan or purpose. The Lord warned men who seek to build, but fail to sit down first and count the cost (Luke 14:28-30). Our Lord used this illustration to show that a bare profession of the gospel, apart from regeneration, would not continue. Not professing high things; but living on high, by the grace of God, brings joy and assurance to the soul of the redeemed. "And hath raised us up together, and made us sit together in heavenly places in Christ Jesus" (Eph. 2:6). The person, who first sits down and counts the cost, is one who considers whether the work of grace is truly wrought in his soul. Profession of faith is costly. It involves self denial, and must expect to suffer the loss of the favor of lost relatives and friends. Now, if our Lord expects this of all who profess to be His followers, what about His own purpose? The foundation of God's plan was laid in eternity by an all-wise Person. The hands which laid the foundation shall raise up the superstructure of that which He planned to accomplish. Neither Satan, nor all his followers, are able to thwart God's eternal purpose. "Declaring the end from the beginning, and from ancient times the things that are not yet done, saying, My counsel shall stand, and I will do all my pleasure" (Is. 46:10). God's planning, therefore, was for His own pleasure. His acts of creation are the result of foreordination, election, and predetermination.

Would man be so foolish as to suggest that God created without a plan? There is a *primary* and *secondary* creation. Primary creation is the act of God when ". . . he commanded, and they were created" (Ps. 148:5). Primary creation must be viewed in the light of Divine intelligence. The creation, which was formed in Divine intelligence, became the external reality by God's absolute power. Secondary creation belongs to the province of providence. Here, again, the Divine intelligence is clearly manifested. We do not deny the laws of nature, but there is in the course of nature a varied and ever varying stream. No two events or objects are exactly alike. This proves that Divine intelligence is actively engaged in the work of providence.

God's creation is for His own pleasure. "For of him, and through him, and to him, are all things: to whom be glory for ever. Amen." (Rom. 11:36). All things are *of God* by creation, *through Him* by providence, and *to Him* by everything being directed to His glory. Therefore, election, redemption, and regeneration all spring from God's sovereign will; they are accomplished by His Divine power, and disposed to His glory. Paul is speaking of everything that comes within the created and providential order. This proves that God did not create for the sake of His own creatures, but for His own glory. "For by him were all things created, that are in heaven, and that are in earth, visible and invisible, whether they be thrones, or dominions, or principalities, or powers; all things were created by him, and for him" (Col. 1:16).

God lives for His own eternal pleasure. Many religionists have the perverted idea that God lives primarily for His creatures, but this is only another illustration of scriptural ignorance. What did God live for before He created? Since God eternally lived to please Himself, did He change after the creation of man? Since creation, does God live for man, or does He continue to live for His own pleasure? God cannot live for any object greater than Himself, for there is no object greater than God. "To whom then will ye liken God? or what likeness will ye compare unto him? . . . To whom then will ye liken me, or shall I be equal? saith the Holy One . . . Hast thou not known? has thou not heard, that the everlasting God, the Lord, the Creator of the ends of the earth, fainteth not, neither is weary? there is no searching of his understanding" (Is. 40:18,25,28). God cannot live for any object lower than Himself because that would make the cause live for the effect.

If God lives for His creatures, as so many advocate, then the greater would be subordinated to the lesser. Once this opinion is adopted, there is no end to its results in this life. This is the doctrine of all false philosophers. They are not only living on a descending scale, but they would have God live on the same descending estimate of life. These persons prefer the physical to the spiritual, the creature to the Creator, and the blessing to the Blesser. This false concept of God makes the infinite Being live for slime. To further illustrate the heresy, it is like saying the sun exists for the dunghill. The conclusion of this philosophy is vividly portrayed in Romans 1:18-32.

The Bible nowhere implies that there are conditions to any of God's creative acts, but the one act with which we are presently interested is regeneration. "For God, who commanded the light to shine out of darkness, hath shined in our hearts, to give the light of the knowledge of the glory of God in the face of Jesus Christ" (II Cor. 4:6). The facts referred to in this text include two great events: (1) *God caused light to shine in the place where natural darkness covered the earth;* and (2) *God caused, by the same word of command, the light of the Holy Spirit to shine in the soul which was totally dark.* His first words, in the regeneration of a soul are, "Let there be light." The Bible is a light which requires light from the Holy Spirit to enable one to see and understand it (I Cor. 2). The light of regeneration is neither the increase of, nor the improvement of the light of nature. It is a new light, created in the understanding of man by the Holy Spirit in regeneration.

The heart of man, by nature, is like the darkness of the earth's surface before God said, "Let there be light." As there was no light upon the face of the chaotic earth before God spoke, so there is no light in the unregenerate heart before God speaks. Without the illumination of the Spirit, in regeneration, there can be no repentance and faith. Thus, the Spirit draws the soul to Christ in regeneration. He then shines in that heart, by conviction of sin that wounds, and then the convicted man embraces Jesus Christ for deliverance. The same powerful word, that caused the light to shine out of darkness, is required to make light shine into the heart of a darkened soul.

Three important metaphors are used to describe the regeneration of the soul. *Creation* is the first; no pre-existent matter is required. "For we are his workmanship, created in Christ Jesus unto good works, which God hath before ordained that we should walk in them" (Eph. 2:10). Where there is no pre-existent matter, there is no opposition. *Resurrection* is the second metaphor; this is the work of omnipotent power. There is pre-existent matter in resurrection. "If ye then be risen with Christ, seek those things which are above, where Christ sitteth on the right hand of God" (Col. 3:1). And, the last metaphor is *conquest.* "(For the weapons of our warfare are not carnal, but mighty through God to the pulling down of strong holds;) Casting down imaginations, and every high thing that exalteth itself against the knowledge of God, and bringing into captivity every thought to obedience of Christ" (II Cor. 10:4,5). Conquest supposes opposition; therefore, the corrupt nature of man, dead in sin, was fully armed against God; but not able to frustrate God's purpose to save him. When regenerated, the rebellious sinner is carried captive, not against his will, but with his will as a voluntary subject of Christ.

Nicodemus continued in ignorance because he was yet unregenerated and unconverted. Divine truths, though told in plainest terms, remain obscure to the natural mind. Carnal reason continues until there is illumination by the Holy Spirit. Hence, Nicodemus asked, ". . . How can these things be?" (John 3:9). Here was a teacher of religion, stumbling over one of the first principles of the doctrine of Christ. This was not the first time the teacher of Israel had asked *how.* To ask *how* of God is a sure sign of unbelief. In the things of God, it is not the *how* but the *who* that counts.

Natural men often admit facts, in the natural realm, as perplexing to them as the new birth is in the spiritual sphere. They do not spend time questioning how the wind cools and refreshes in the summer, levels the giant oak during a storm, and lashes the sea into a foam during a hurricane. It matters little *how* these things are accomplished; the important thing is, they are performed. But when it comes to spiritual realities, depraved men want to know the *how* of things as did Nicodemus. This is only a manifestation of their depravity.

It is a greater sin for religious teachers to be ignorant of Divine truth because of their position. Our Lord condemned the masters of Israel, when He said, ". . . Every plant, which my heavenly Father hath not planted, shall be rooted up. Let them alone: they be blind leaders of the blind. And if the blind lead the blind, both shall fall into the ditch" (Matt. 15:13,14). They were blind as to the Person of the Messiah, regeneration, and the gospel of Christ. Isaiah predicted that there would be blind teachers at the time the Divine Logos should tabernacle among them. ". . . Who is blind, but my servant? . . . who is blind as he that is perfect, and blind as the Lord's servant? Seeing many things, but thou observest not; opening the ears, but he heareth not" (Is. 42:17-20). These leaders possessed nothing more than what they had from nature, or had attained at the school of the prophets. They were blind leaders leading blind people, and their destination was the ditch of ignorance, despair, and eternal destruction.

JESUS CHRIST IS THE REVEALER OF REGENERATION

The discourse between Christ and Nicodemus illustrates an important principle which should be observed by every witness for the Son of God. Christ took the very statements made by Nicodemus and turned them upon the unregenerate teacher.

1. Nicodemus declared, ". . . *we know* thou art a teacher come from God . . ." (John 3:2). The Jews knew that the Messiah was to be a teacher. "And it shall come to pass in the last days, that the mountain of the Lord's house shall be established . . . and he will teach us of his ways, and we will walk in his paths: for out of Zion shall go forth the law, and the word of the Lord from Jerusalem" (Is. 2:2,3). "Thus saith the Lord, thy Redeemer, the Holy One of Israel; I am the Lord thy God which teacheth thee to profit, which leadeth thee by the way that thou shouldest go" (Is. 48:17). It is possible for men to have knowledge of such things; and, yet, be unaffected by what they know. Nicodemus said, "We know," but he was the only one who came to Christ. Men, who come short of the knowledge of salvation, may have high thoughts of Christ.

Christ said, ". . . We speak that *we do know*, and testify that we have seen; and ye receive not our witness" (John 3:11). Our Lord, in reply to Nicodemus in verse 2 said, *We* who are engaged in preaching the truth know what we are proclaiming. There is some discussion as to whom the plural pronoun *we* refers. Some think it refers to the Godhead, the Father Who was ever with Christ, and the Spirit Who anointed Him to preach the gospel. Others think that the plural pronoun refers to the Old Testament prophets, John the Baptist, and Christ Himself. It really does not matter, the important thing is that those who were sent to preach knew what they were proclaiming. There is a real warning in this for every preacher and teacher. He is required to know, not only mentally but experimentally, what he is seeking to diffuse.

The Lord Jesus also stated, *We have seen.* Christ saw through His omniscient eye all the operations of the Spirit on the hearts of men, and His servants saw the effects of the regenerating Spirit in the changed lives of men. They were able to see the effects of regeneration as they saw the effects of the wind.

Knowing and *seeing* are qualifications of a witness for the Lord. "These things have I written unto you that believe on the name of the Son of God; that ye may know that ye have eternal life, and that ye may believe on the name of the Son of God" (I John 5:13). ". . . I have appeared unto thee for this purpose, to make thee a minister and a witness both of these things which thou hast seen, and of those things in the which I will appear unto thee" (Acts 26:16). The eternal Son manifested great condescension by including men with Himself, in the same yoke of bearing witness to the truth of the gospel. Though these men often make mistakes about the truths committed to their trust, the truths themselves are infallible. John the Baptist, for example, was a witness of Jesus Christ (John 3:23-36). But who would say that John's knowledge was as perfect as Christ's?

The climax of Christ's reply to Nicodemus was, "Ye receive not our witness" (John 3:11). This proves that Nicodemus was yet in his sins. The strongest external evidence of truth's confirmation does not affect the unregenerate heart. The Spirit alone can confirm the truth of the gospel internally. Thus, the subjective confirmation of objective truth is the work of the Holy Spirit. A man may witness the conversion of many regenerated people, but he himself will never receive the witness until a work of grace is wrought in his heart.

2. Nicodemus said, "Thou are *a teacher*" (John 3:2). The prophesies concerning *teacher* were known to Nicodemus, but his ignorance is displayed in the statement, "Thou art *a teacher*." The eternal Son of God was more than a teacher, He was *the Teacher* —the Teacher of all teachers, as He is the Lord of lords and King of kings.

The Lord Jesus said to Nicodemus, ". . . Art thou a master (teacher) of Israel, and knowest not these things?" (John 3:10). Nicodemus was not a common teacher; he was a teacher in their great Sanhedrin. Though his fame was known all over Jerusalem and Judea, he was ignorant of the first and most important point in religion. His circumcision of the flesh did not effect the circumcision of his heart. "For in Christ Jesus neither circumcision availeth any thing, nor uncircumcision, but a new creature" (Gal. 6:15).

Men may have much learning, and be teachers of religion;

and, yet, be ignorant of regeneration. What a tragedy it is for men to be teachers of God's word, and be strangers of the Incarnate Word, Whom the Scriptures proclaim. Is it surprising that a person, whose business it was to instruct others, should be a stranger to a doctrine as clearly revealed in the Old Testament as the new birth? "And I will give them one heart, and I will put a new spirit within you; and I will take the stony heart out of their flesh, and will give them an heart of flesh" (Ezek. 11:19). "Then will I sprinkle clean water upon you, and ye shall be clean: from all your filthiness, and from all your idols, will I cleanse you. A new heart also will I give you, and a new spirit will I put within you: and I will take away the stony heart out of your flesh, and I will give you an heart of flesh" (Ezek. 36:25,26). The Bible constantly warns about false prophets and teachers (Jer. 5:31; 6:30). When teachers have been tried and found wanting, they are called *reprobate silver*. This was confirmed by the Lord's rejection of them as being those whom He had called and sent. The one great business of teachers is to know the way of salvation.

3. Nicodemus said, ". . . no man can do these miracles that thou doest, except God be with him" (John 3:2). He was speaking of the miracles Christ performed at the Passover in Jerusalem. Miracles were expected to be wrought by the Messiah; but Nicodemus, not knowing that this was the true Messiah, thought He was nothing more than a man. This is all that men, who claim that Jesus Christ was peccable, see in Him today.

The Lord Jesus answered Nicodemus by saying, ". . . Except a man be born again, he cannot see the kingdom of God" (John 3:3). Regeneration of the soul, which includes the impartation of the faculty of faith, is required to be able to penetrate the human nature of Jesus Christ and behold the impeccable Person of the Divine Son of God.

The spiritual blindness of Nicodemus is seen in the fact that he acknowledged Jesus Christ as only a teacher, not Saviour. There are many teachers of religion today, who see no more in Jesus Christ than Nicodemus did when he came to Him by night.

4. Nicodemus asked, ". . . How can a man be born when he is old?... (John 3:4). The natural mind of the teacher of Israel

is brought to light by this question. There is quite a difference between nature and grace. Nature declares the glory of God's power and wisdom, objectively (Ps. 19:1-6; Rom. 1:19,20); but grace applies the redemption wrought out by Jesus Christ, subjectively.

Psalm 19 gives three aspects of revelation: (1) *Natural,* in creation (vs. 1-6); (2) *Revealed,* in Scripture (vs. 7-11); and (3) *Experimental,* by grace (vs. 12-14).

Christ answered, ". . . Except a man be born again . . . born of water and the Spirit . . ." (John 3:3,5), he can neither see nor enter the kingdom of God. The new birth is wrought by the Holy Spirit, and this is accomplished like water cleansing from filth (Ezek. 36:25,26).

As in the natural birth a new creature is brought forth, so in regeneration a new nature is communicated to the recipient of grace. Regeneration is not patching up the old nature, but imparting a new nature. When a child is brought into this world, it is invested with properties and dispositions agreeable to the nature that begat it. Thus, in regeneration, there is a new principle of life endued with properties and dispositions agreeable to the nature of God. Every baby is sensible to things contrary to its life, and every born again person is sensitive to things contrary to grace. There is a visible relation between every child and his parents, and there is a visible manifestation of the grace of union in the life of every person born of the Spirit.

5. Nicodemus asked, ". . . *can he enter* the second time into his mother's womb, and be born?" (John 3:4). This question conveys a great perplexity in the teacher of Israel. His ignorance made him look upon the new birth as something impossible.

Christ replies that Nicodemus cannot enter into the kingdom except by the new birth. *Seeing* the kingdom is by the exercise of the faculty of faith, planted in regeneration. *Entering* the kingdom will take place when it is established. "Wherefore the rather, brethren, give diligence to make your calling and election sure: for if ye do these things, ye shall never fall: For so an entrance shall be ministered unto you abundantly into the everlasting kingdom of our Lord and Saviour Jesus Christ" (II Pet. 1:10,11).

6. Nicodemus asked, ". . . How can these things be?" (John 3:9). The natural reason of depraved man is conquered only by the truth of God applied by the Spirit. "(For the weapons of our warfare are not carnal, but mighty through God to the pulling down of strong holds;) Casting down imaginations and every high thing that exalteth itself against the knowledge of God, and bringing into captivity every thought to the obedience of Christ . . ." (II Cor. 10:4-6). The *strong holds* are sin, Satan, unbelief, pride, hardness of heart, etc. The imaginations of the mind are silenced and conquered by applied truth. Thoughts are brought to the obedience of Christ. The enlightened soul looks to Christ for salvation, embraces Him and His truths, and obeys from a heart made willing by the Spirit.

Christ asked, "If I have told you of earthly things, and ye believe not, *how shall ye believe*, if I tell you of heavenly things?" (John 3:12). This does not mean that the truths He delivered were earthly, but He had presented heavenly things in the most suitable manner for a lost man. Spiritual things, when presented in terms of earthly similitudes, are but earthly things in comparison to what they actually are if presented in heavenly language. There is an immanency in spiritual things which can never be expressed by the use of earthly similitudes. As the essential glory of God had to be veiled in human nature, for man to be able to see and handle the Word of life; so spiritual truths had to be expressed in similitudes for man's understanding. The operations of the Spirit are set forth under the symbol of the wind.

7. Nicodemus asked, ". . . How can these things be?" (John 3:9). There are legitimate questions, but the question by Nicodemus was an objection to the possibility of such a birth. Water, Spirit, and wind all seemed confusing to his natural mind.

Christ asked, ". . . Art thou a master (teacher) of Israel, and knowest not these things?" (John 3:10). Our Lord rebuked Nicodemus for his ignorance because of his position as teacher of Israel. What hope of eternal life does man have apart from the regenerating work of the Spirit of God?

The Lord Jesus concludes His discourse with Nicodemus on the subject of the new birth. "And no man hath ascended up to heaven, but he that came down from heaven, even the Son of man which is in heaven" (John 3:13). He showed the teacher of Israel that no man can ascend to heaven and learn heavenly things, then return to earth to instruct men. That prerogative belongs to the second Person of the Godhead, for it was the Lord Jesus Who came down from heaven for the purpose of declaring the Father. "No man hath seen God at any time; the only begotten Son, which is in the bosom of the Father, he hath declared him" (John 1:18). Christ did not bring His human nature from heaven, but as the Divine Person, He assumed human nature when He came to earth. At the same time He was on earth in His human nature, He was in heaven in His Divine nature. The assumption of human nature into union with His Divine Person did not destroy His omnipresence, infinity, or immensity. The Lord Jesus Christ did not cease to be what He eternally was, but He did assume that which He did not eternally possess—a human nature.

The phrase, ". . . no man hath ascended up to heaven . . ." (John 3:13), is not to be understood absolutely. Elijah, the prophet, ascended up to heaven before the Lord Jesus, but his ascension was by God's power. Christ alone had the power to go to heaven and bring back knowledge of heavenly things. No person ever ascended into heaven for that purpose, but the Son of Man Who is in heaven. Since Nicodemus had acknowledged Christ to be a teacher come from God, our Lord would have Nicodemus, a teacher of Israel, to know that He was the only perfect Teacher of heavenly things. Only the Lord of heaven could teach such heavenly truths. "It is not in heaven, that thou shouldest say, Who shall go up for us to heaven, and bring it unto us, that we may hear it, and do it?" (Deut. 30:12). "But the righteousness which is of faith speaketh on this wise, Say not in thine heart, Who shall ascend into heaven? (that is, to bring Christ down from above)" (Rom. 10:6).

Agur gives us a wonderful prophecy. "Who hath ascended up into heaven, or descended? who hath gathered the wind in his fists? who hath bound the waters in a garment? who hath established all the ends of the earth? what is his name, and what is his son's name, if thou canst tell?" (Prov. 30:4). What is his name? God is above all names because He is infinite. Infinity, therefore, cannot be measured by names. What is His Son's name? Christ has many names in the holy Scriptures. The names given to Him reveal a clear distinction of the Persons of the Godhead.

The Son, however, is co-equal and co-eternal with the Father (Matt. 11:27; John 14:7-9; Heb. 1:3). Who is able to tell? "All things are delivered unto me of my Father: and no man knoweth the Son, but the Father; neither knoweth any man the Father, save the Son, and he to whomsoever the Son will reveal him" (Matt. 11:27). The mirror in which we behold the Father and the Son is found in the verse quoted from Proverbs 30:4.

It is as impossible for men, in their natural condition, to comprehend spiritual mysteries as for one to climb up to heaven and enter into God's secret counsel. There is a sense, however, in which a man born of the Spirit ascends to understand spiritual things. Christ, however, is showing Nicodemus that only the Mediator between God and man has direct access to heaven. Thus, the Lord Jesus, by His incarnation, did not cease to be God; but continues to fill heaven and earth for the purpose of infallibly teaching man.

The Son of God, in the bosom of the Father, was pleased to condescend to manifest Himself unto the world in human nature. Scripture makes clear the fact that Jesus Christ is a Divine Person; His Person is eternal and changeless, whether subsisting in the "form of God" (Phil. 2:6), or "come in the flesh" (I John 4:2). He is the same forever, and has a Divine title conveying the thought of eternal immutability (Heb. 13:8). In the beginning, He was with God and He was God. He is *I Am;* His ". . . goings forth have been from of old, from everlasting" (Micah 5:2).

The glory of Christ's eternal Person is vividly portrayed in the gospel according to John. We are greatly impressed, as we read the gospel according to John, by the statements which declare the personal greatness and glory of the One sent by the Father. He who comes from above is above all. "He that cometh from above is above all: he that is of the earth is earthly, and speaketh of the earth: he that cometh from heaven is above all" (John 3:31).

The Person of Jesus Christ is unchanged in the incarnation. Whatever place, service, or relationship Christ assumed to accomplish, God's eternal purpose made no change in His Person. There are many references, in the gospel according to John, where Jesus Christ speaks of Himself as *the sent one.* The word *sent* implies a *relative* position, which is not one of absolute equality. It implies authority on the part of the Sender, and subjection on the part of the One sent. We cannot think of Jesus Christ, as God, assuming a place of subjection. God, absolutely considered, cannot be in subjection to anyone; but Jesus Christ, as the sent One from the Father, is under authority. He was in a subordinate relation to the One Who sent Him.

If we do not distinguish between the Mediatorial glory of Jesus Christ, as the sent One; and the proper glory of His Person, as God absolutely considered, we shall lose something of the true character of both. The Mediatorial glory of Jesus Christ derives its luster from His Personal glory, but to make His Mediatorial glory the full measure of His Personal glory is derogatory to Deity. Thus, the Lord Jesus Christ, as the *Son of Man*, was sent by the Father for the purpose of declaring the Father. The word *sent* indicates His Mediatorial place as the Son of Man. "Wherefore when he cometh into the world, he saith, Sacrifice and offering thou wouldest not, but a body hast thou prepared me: In burnt offerings and sacrifices for sin thou hast had no pleasure. Then said I, Lo, I come (in the volume of the book it is written of me,) to do thy will, O God" (Heb. 10:5-7).

Jesus Christ was eternally God; but as the Son of God, in Manhood, He is said to be *sent* and *given*. No man ever called Jesus Christ the *Son of Man* during the days of His flesh on earth. This title is applied to the Lord Jesus only three times by others in all the Scriptures (Acts 7:56; Rev. 1:13; 14:14). The title *Son of Man* is used many times in the New Testament; this was Christ's own designation for Himself. In several notable instances, the title *Son of Man* is used in connection with Divine undertakings; in like manner, the title, *Son of God* is used a few times in association with human features. Thus, the Son of God assumed human nature into such union that what is proper to either nature is ascribed to the Person under whatever name He chose to call Himself. "And no man hath ascended up to heaven, but he that came down from heaven, even the Son of man which is in heaven" (John 3:13). "And the angel answered and said unto her, The Holy Ghost shall come upon thee, and the power of the Highest shall overshadow thee: therefore also that holy thing which shall be born of thee shall be called the Son of God" (Luke 1:35).

The position of man, as such, is inferior to God, and is always presented that way in the Scriptures. The great mystery of the incarnation is, that in self humiliation and by descent of infinite love, Jesus Christ took the position of Man, which is lower than the position that eternally belongs to Him as God. He was as perfect in the inferior position of *form of servant* as He was in the *form of God*. "Who being in the form of God, thought it not robbery to be equal with God: But made himself of no reputation, and took upon him the form of a servant, and was made in the likeness of men" (Phil. 2:6,7). It could not be otherwise if we think of Who it was Who became Man. As to His Person, He is **eternally Divine**; but in becoming Man, He has come into a place which, in itself, is inferior to the place and condition of Deity. But, in Person, He is all that He ever was; thus, He is, even as Man, God's fellow. "Awake, O sword, against my shepherd, and against the man that is my fellow, saith the Lord of hosts: smite the shepherd, and the sheep shall be scattered: and I will turn mine hand upon the little ones" (Zech. 13:7).

The word *inferior*, when used in connection with the Lord, applies to the position taken and not the Person who took it. If we do not admit His coming into a lower or inferior position, in becoming Man, we have lost the meaning of the incarnation. It must be clearly understood, that neither the Son nor the Holy Spirit is subordinate in Deity. Such a thought would be heresy. But they both have been pleased to take a subordinate place in the economy of revelation. The Son of God, as well as the Holy Spirit, is God in the most absolute sense. But the Son and the Spirit have been pleased to take a relative position, which is not commensurate with their full personal glory. The Son in Manhood is viewed in a subordinate position, fulfilling the will of God the Father. The Holy Spirit is also revealed, occupying a subordinate place; He does not speak of Himself but of that which glorifies the Son (John 16:7-14). Both the Son and the Spirit render their wonderful service in order to make known the Father.

God, as Father, has been made known by the Son. Our knowledge of God, revealed by the holy name of *Father*, is dependent on the incarnation. Hence, Divine names and titles are used in Scripture to identify the Persons. Jesus Christ was not *actually* the Son of Man before the incarnation, but the Person Who is now revealed as the Son of Man was from eternity; and He is now ascended up where He was before. "What and if ye shall see the Son of man ascend up where he was before?" (John 6:62). As God told Moses (Ex. 6:3) that He was not made known to Abraham, Isaac, and Jacob by the name Jehovah; so God the Father and Jesus

Christ were not actually revealed by those names until the incarnation.

In Ephesians 1:3, God is spoken of as The God and Father of our Lord Jesus Christ, Who chose us in Christ before the foundation of the world. Every thoughtful Christian knows that God could not be the God of another Divine Person, when both are absolute Deity. But Jesus Christ, having come in the flesh, could say, "My Father and my God." He was in the position of a Man relative to God, and the Son in relation to God the Father. "The God and Father of our Lord Jesus Christ" is God, as He is known in relation to Jesus Christ in His Mediatorial capacity. The Persons of the Godhead are eternally the same, though in Divine wisdom they may be known by names which were not publicly revealed in Old Testament times. We know Divine Persons only when they are made known to us by names which we can understand.

There is a progressive revelation of God to man in the Scriptures. In the Old Testament, God was pleased to be known by certain names, which gave character to the knowledge and faith of His people. The people could not go beyond what was made known of God in those names. The patriarchs did not know God by the name of Jehovah, and the Old Testament saints did not know Him by the name of Father. God's name is the way He is pleased to be known by men, and it has always been in keeping with what they have needed for support in any given time. We know Him now as the *Father*, but He was not revealed in Old Testament times as such. Knowledge of Him was formed by other names. We cannot carry the names *Father* and *Son*, as they are used in the New Testament, back into the Old Testament Scriptures. The reverence for God as Father was held in reserve until the incarnation of Jesus Christ.

The relationship of a father and a son offers an interesting study in the Scriptures. We find that a son is at the disposal of his father. "And he said, Take now thy son, thine only son Isaac, whom thou lovest, and get thee into the land of Moriah; and offer him there for a burnt offering upon one of the mountains which I will tell thee of" (Gen. 22:2). "Thou shalt not delay to offer the first of thy ripe fruits, and of thy liquors: the firstborn of thy sons shalt thou give unto me" (Ex. 22:29). He is to harken to his father who begat him, and to hear his instruction (Prov.

1:8; 23:22). A man's son is born unto him as a subject of care (Deut. 1:31). A father is to command his son and to require obedience of him; a son is to honor, reverence, and serve his father (Ex. 20:12; Lev. 19:3; Mal. 1:6; 3:17). A father is to chasten his son when necessary (Deut. 8:5; Heb. 12:5-11). These Scriptures prove, that while the relationship of father and son are associated, they are never regarded as being co-equal. To suppose that they are is to throw the whole structure of Scriptural thought into confusion. If a son refused to harken to the voice of his father, it was so great an evil in the sight of the father that the penalty was death (Deut. 21:18-21).

The relationship between God the Father and His Son Jesus Christ is quite different from earthly relationships of father and son. The Son of God was, in every way, holy, sinless, and perfect. He never knew corrective chastening as the sons of men so constantly experience. Every feature of sonship, which the Old Testament brings out, was found to perfection in Jesus Christ. He was begotten of God, the subject of the Father's love and care, and ever in subjection to the Father's will. He always honored and served His Father (Heb. 10:7). The gospel of John clearly and fully reveals these characteristics of the Lord Jesus Christ, the second Person of the Godhead. Jesus Christ was constantly in the place of obedience, receiving instruction from the Father as to what He should say and do. He even stated, ". . . The Son can do nothing of himself . . ." (John 5:19). He received everything from the Father; He was ever under the Father's commandment and the object of the Father's love. All that God desired in a son was in Jesus Christ. The Lord Jesus had a subordinate place for the purpose of fulfilling God's eternal decree. Even in the place of subjection the Lord Jesus could say, "I and my Father are one" (John 10:30). The Jews understood that anyone, who could say that God was his own father, made himself equal with God. "Therefore the Jews sought the more to kill him, because he not only had broken the sabbath, but said also that God was his Father, making himself equal with God" (John 5:18). Therefore, they took up stones to stone Him because He made Himself equal with God.

There are some theologians who believe in the Divine Triunity, but have some strange views concerning the names of *Father* and *Son*. They emphasize that such expressions as *eternal generation*, and *eternal Sonship* should never be used. They maintain that these expressions involve the serious error that in some way the Deity of the Son is derived or communicated from the Father, and is, therefore, of subordinate character. They also maintain that theologians of the past, failing to see that the word *begotten* refers to Jesus Christ as the One born of the virgin in time, tried to escape the difficulty by inventing unscriptural phrases of *eternal generation* and *eternal Sonship*.

Answers to the objections to *eternal generation* and *eternal Sonship* might seem difficult to many, but the student of Scripture finds the answers very simple. For instance, the word *generation* means individuals having equal status at the same time. This simply means that both Father and Son have always been co-equal and co-eternal. The simplest answer to these objections is that there never was a time when the thought of Father and Son were not in the mind of God. In reality, it is a denial of the infinite understanding of God (Ps. 147:5). God knows future, present, and past all at once; He is one mind. "But he is in one mind, and who can turn him? and what his soul desireth, even that he doeth" (Job 23:13). There is no succession in God's knowledge and understanding, but there is in man's. God's knowledge is from eternity; He is before and above time. God knows all things by one act of intuition; there is no division in His knowledge.

God's name of *Father* was not revealed until there was a Divine Person on earth, as Man, to declare Him (John 1:18; Matt. 11:27). The Son of God, as the Divine Person in Manhood, spoke of the glory He had with the Father before the foundation of the world (John 17:5,24). Glory, which He had with the Father before the foundation of the world, was a glory proper to His eternal Person. He descended from the glory, which He had with the Father, for the purpose of completing the work given Him to perform. A Divine Person could not remain in humiliation; thus, after finishing the work the Father sent Him to perform, He ascended back to the Father. He is now glorified, as Man, with the Father; and the glory which He has with the Father is the same glory He had with Him before the world was.

The Deity of Jesus Christ is asserted in Hebrews, chapter one. It is in Manhood that God spoke by Jesus Christ. And, as Man, He set Himself down on the right hand of the Majesty on high. As Man, God addressed Him as His Son. As Man, He was brought into the habitable world as firstborn and worshipped by all God's angels. As Man, He will have the millennial throne and sceptre. But this Man is God, and is addressed as God; His eternal Deity is unquestionable. The subject of Hebrews 1:5-13 is the greatness and Deity of the Messiah, God's anointed Man as prophesied in the Old Testament Scriptures.

Let us now consider the main objection to the statement of Christ's eternal Sonship. Some devoted Trinitarians take the position that the second Person of the Godhead is known to us as having become Man, and bearing the title of *Son* in Manhood. They assert that Scripture speaks of the *eternal Spirit* (Heb. 9:14), but this does not justify the position of those who speak of Christ as the *eternal Son*. They also state that the fact of advancing such an argument soon finds difficulty in securing a Scriptural foundation. Thus, they say, the use of the word *eternal* in the epistle to the Hebrews contrasts what God has brought in now, through Christ and His death, with what was known in Judaism. Their argument concludes by stating, "The Spirit is not a name of relationship like Father and Son. The Spirit has not been manifested like the Son, or revealed like the Father. He remains in His eternal character as the unseen Spirit; and can, therefore, be spoken of as 'eternal Spirit.' But Spirit does not speak of the 'eternal Father' or 'the eternal Son' because the Father and Son are names which give character to our present knowledge of God. They are names which can be known only through the incarnation." Again, they state, "We do not think that any Scripture can be adduced that applies the title 'Son' or 'Son of God,' to our Lord Jesus Christ as Deity in the past eternity. Scripture teaches unquestionably that His Person is eternal; it invariably attaches these titles to Him whether prophetically or actually, as in Manhood."

To everyone who believes that Jesus Christ is truly God, as well as truly Man, His word on Manhood and Sonship is final. Christ said to the two men going to Emmaus "And beginning at Moses and all the prophets, he expounded unto them in all the scriptures the things concerning himself" (Luke 24:27). The whole force of the argument lies in the fact that Jesus Christ regarded Moses, not as a mere title by which certain books were known, but as the instrument used of God in giving both history and prophesy concerning the Lord Jesus Christ. Christ said to the Jews, "For had ye believed Moses, ye would have believed me: for he wrote of me. But if ye believe not his writings, how shall ye believe my words?" (John 5 :46,47).

Jesus Christ is the God-Man, Son to both. When Jesus Christ said, ". . . Abraham rejoiced to see my day: and he saw it, and was glad" (John 8:56), He had reference to the day the Son of Man should be revealed. As the Son of God He has no day; as the Son of Man He was revealed. We are told that even in the days of Christ's flesh, He continued still a Son. "Though he were a Son, yet learned he obedience by the things which he suffered" (Heb. 5 :8). The Lord Jesus was not a Son by creation, adoption, or office; He was a Son by nature, being the only begotten of the Father and having the same nature and perfection as the Father.

Genealogies of Jesus Christ were given by Matthew and Luke. Both give a long genealogy showing our Lord's ancestry. Matthew places his at the beginning of his letter; Luke does not give his until after the Lord's baptism in Jordan. The first important thing with Matthew was to establish our Lord's Davidic lineage; Luke's concern was the real human birth and growth through Boyhood to Youth to Manhood. The pedigree of our Lord, as given by Luke, ends with a wonderful leap from earth to heaven. Matthew gives the genealogy through Joseph who was legally, though not actually, the father of Jesus. Luke gives it through Mary, who was really mother of His Manhood. Matthew's genealogy comes down from Abraham to Jesus Christ, while Luke goes from Jesus Christ to Adam, and to God. The reason for the two views of the genealogies is: (1) The Jew found the basis of his thought in a revelation which proceeds from cause to effect; and (2) The Greek possessed nothing beyond the fact, and he proceeded from effect to cause.

The first occurrence in the New Testament of the full title *the Son of God* is found in Peter's confession (Matt. 16 :16). Was this confession due to the sudden appreciation of the fact that the Lord's mother was a virgin? That truth could be attested by flesh and blood on the recognized principles of evidence; but, of His Sonship, the Lord declared it was the *revelation of heaven.* "And Jesus answered and said unto him, Blessed art thou, Simon Bar-jona: for flesh and blood hath not revealed it unto thee, but my Father which is in heaven" (Matt. 16:17). "Whosoever shall confess that Jesus is the Son of God, God dwelleth in him, and he in God" (I John 4 :15). By the title, *Son of Man,* Jesus Christ claimed to be Man in the highest and most absolute sense; and, by the title *Son of God* He laid claim to Deity.

As there is more than one Person in the Godhead, so there is a distinction between *God* and *Lord God* (Gen. 1:26; 2:4). This is not, according to Luke 24:27, an arbitrary or unauthorized interpretation of the Old Testament Scriptures. It cannot be denied, that in God's image, man somehow represents God. God said, when He created man, ". . . Let us make man in our image, after our likeness . . ." (Gen. 1:26). The word *image* means that man was fitted with certain capacities as God's representative. The word *likeness* means that man, before the fall, was blessed with a tendency Godward. In Genesis, chapter one, you will notice the uniform word for the Almighty is *God* (Elohim). But, when you come to chapter two, a new name is introduced (2:4). It is no longer God, but *Lord God*. This change is significant. When Moses advances to the creation of man he reveals a more intimate side of the Divine Character. *Lord* is the name which means Owner, Possessor; One who treasures and cherishes, Whose affections center upon what He has made. In chapter one the emphasis is on creation in power. Now, it is creation in love, and the word changes from God to Lord God; a gracious sovereign Preserver, Protector, and Benefactor. The name *Lord* refers to the second Person of the Godhead Who at this point discloses Himself.

God the Father has been seen by no man, but God the Son constantly appeared as the Jehovah of the Old Testament. There must be a progressive revelation of God to man because of man's natural limitations. The Old Testament is a record of that progressive revelation. The Lord Jesus is God's last word to man (Heb. 1:1-3). Jehovah first appears in Genesis 2:4 as the God of providence. The next occurrence is related to the creation of man (Gen. 2:7). God's dealings with man, in connection with kindness and love, come through Jehovah. It was Jehovah Who announced the Redeemer (Gen. 3:15), accepted Abel's offering (Gen. 4), gave Noah the pattern of the ark (Gen. 6), demanded the sacrifice of passover (Ex. 12), and gave the law at Sinai (Ex. 19; 20). It is by this significant introduction of the Divine name *Lord God* that we are led to apprehend the true nobility of man as the offspring and product of Divine forethought and affection.

He, Who was promised to Adam as the seed of the woman (Gen. 3:15), was declared to be the seed of Abraham (Gal. 3:16). The

Scripture plainly states that it was not through the children of Abraham, as a nation, but through Christ that all the nations of the earth were to be blessed. Thus, Abraham saw the day of Christ and was glad. Jesus Christ said, ". . . Before Abraham was, I am" (John 8:58). This proves that the Person predicted as the seed of the woman and the seed of Abraham—the One through Whom redemption was to be accomplished—was to be both God and Man. He could not be the seed of Abraham if He was not a Man, and He could not be the Saviour of men unless He is God.

In Genesis 22, God commanded Abraham to offer up Isaac as a sacrifice. The Angel of Jehovah arrested his hand at the moment of sacrifice and said, ". . . now I know that thou fearest God, seeing that thou hast not withheld thy son, thine only son from me" (Gen. 22:12). The Angel of the Lord also said, ". . . By myself have I sworn, saith the Lord, for because thou hast done this thing, and hast not withheld thy son, thine only son: That in blessing I will bless thee, and in multiplying I will multiply thy seed as the stars of the heaven . . ." (Gen. 22:16,17). And Abraham called the name of that place Jehovah-jireh. The Angel of Jehovah and Jehovah are names given to the same Person, who swears by Himself and promises the blessing of a numerous posterity to Abraham. The Angel of Jehovah, therefore, is a Divine Person.

In Exodus 3, we have the account of the revelation of God to Moses on Mount Horeb. The Angel of the Lord appeared to Moses at the burning bush. The Angel is identical with Jehovah and is declared to be the God of Abraham, Isaac, and Jacob. The personal distinction between Jehovah and the Angel of Jehovah (i. e., between the Father and the Son, as these Persons are elsewhere in the New Testament Scriptures, designated), is clearly presented in Exodus 23:20,21. "Behold, I send an Angel before thee, to keep thee in the way, and to bring thee into the place which I have prepared. Beware of him, and obey his voice, provoke him not; he will not pardon your transgressions: for my name is in him." The last phrase is equivalent to, *I am in Him. The name of God,* often means God Himself as manifested. Thus, it is said of the temple, ". . . My name shall be there . . ." (I Kings 8:29), i. e., *there will I dwell.*

Who can deny that Psalms 2, 22, 45, 72, and 110 are Messianic? Both the major and minor prophets are filled with predictions concerning the *birth of a Child, Branch of Jehovah, Ruler of Israel, Ancient of days,* and *Messenger of the covenant.* (Is. 7-9; Micah 5; Jer. 23; Dan. 2; 7; Mal. 3). Since the prophecies of Isaiah 9:6 preceded the incarnation, how foolish to say that Sonship is not eternal. The prophecy of Isaiah states, "For unto us a child is born, unto us a son is given. . . ." The child is *born,* refers to the seed of David; but the Son *given,* refers to the eternal Sonship of Jesus Christ. The elect of God were chosen in the Lord Jesus Christ before the foundation of the world (Eph. 1:3-14) ; therefore, the name Son was eternally in the mind of God the Father.

Four factors are absolutely necessary to understand the Person of Jesus Christ: (1) He was truly human, so that everything that can be declared of Man as Man—not of man as fallen—can be proclaimed of Him. (2) He was truly Divine so that everything that can be asserted of God can be affirmed of Him. (3) The human and Divine natures were united in one Person, but Christ did not have a double personality. (4) The two natures in the one Person of Christ were inseparably united, yet they were not mingled, or confounded. Jesus Christ was both Son of God and Son of Man. Such designations imply at once a heavenly preexistence, a present humiliation, and a future glory. The two natures of Jesus Christ must never be thought of as being distinct and separate in Him. The relation must remain to us a mystery, but the evidence of each is abundant, and the necessity for both is obvious. Had He not been Man, He could not have sympathized with us. And had He not been God, He could not have saved us.

The eternal Son, in becoming Man, descended an infinite distance to reach man's highest conceivable exaltation. We must not, however, fail to understand the difference between the Son of Man and other men. These differences concern both origin and absolute sinlessness. Men are of the earth, earthy; but Jesus Christ is from heaven (I Cor. 15:47). Even though Christ was born of woman like other men, yet He descended from heaven. "And no man hath ascended up to heaven, but he that came down from heaven, even the Son of man which is in heaven" (John 3:13). This does not mean that He was already in heaven, as Man; but even though He was, at that time, the Son of Man, He derived His origin from heaven. If Jesus Christ came into the world like all other men, then He is like all other men. He must differ from men in His origin or He cannot be their Saviour.

REGENERATION IS THE FIRST WORK OF GRACE IN REDEMPTION'S APPLICATION

In concluding our discourse on regeneration, I submit twenty-five arguments to prove that regeneration is the first work of grace in redemption's application.

1. *Regeneration* is the implanting of the principle of life by which the call is heard, and Jesus Christ is recognized. "The hearing ear, and the seeing eye, the Lord hath made even both of them" (Prov. 20:12). An unregenerate person is deaf and blind.

2. Every operation of saving grace must be preceded by a *quickening* of the sinner. "And you hath he quickened, who were dead in trespasses and sins" (Eph. 2:1). This quickening (regeneration) unstops deaf ears and opens blind eyes.

3. Sinners need nothing to predispose (give an inclination or tendency beforehand, to render subject) them for the implanting of new life; it is God Who quickens.

4. God's act of giving life to the spiritually dead is distinct from the call of the gospel, just as the faculty of seeing is distinct from light.

5. Regeneration is an immediate and creative act of God, and no instrumental or secondary causes are connected with it.

6. He that is effectually called must be able to *hear* and *come* to Christ, and he is made able by regeneration.

7. The effectual call addresses itself to conscious life; therefore, the call comes from without; but regeneration works from within. But does not the word of God sometimes work in a creative way? (Gen. 1:3; Ps. 33:6,9; 147:15; Rom. 4:17). Answer: These passages refer to the word of God's power, to His authoritative command, and not to the word of preaching. "And when I passed by thee, and saw thee polluted in thine own blood, I said unto thee when thou wast in thy blood, Live; yea, I said unto thee when thou wast in thy blood, Live" (Ezek. 16:6).

8. The *faculty* (spiritual ability) of faith is implanted in regeneration, but its exercise is brought forth in conversion. Men, by nature, have not the faculty or ability; it is the gift of God. "For unto you it is given in the behalf of Christ, not only to believe on him, but also to suffer for his sake" (Phil. 1:29).

"For by grace are ye saved through faith; and that not of yourselves: it is the gift of God" (Eph. 2:8). "And that we may be delivered from unreasonable and wicked men: for all men have not faith" (II Thess. 3:2).

9. Regeneration changes the *soil of the heart* before the *word of the gospel* finds lodgement (Matt. 13:3-9,18-23). This does not imply that the natural faculties are completely insensitive to the word of the gospel. Consider the *stony* and *thorny* ground hearers! Persons may have human understanding of Divine things.

10. Regeneration gives sight to the spiritually blind. In the case of the blind, there is plenty of light; but that which is lacking is sight. What is light to a blind man? (See Mark 10:46-52.) This same principle applies to the dead, deaf, or impotent.

11. The word of the Spirit in regeneration cannot be resisted. Resistance of the Spirit, by man, pertains only to the external (objective) dispensation of grace by the word. "Ye stiff-necked and uncircumcised in heart and ears, ye do always resist the Holy Ghost: as your fathers did, so do ye" (Acts 7:51). Contrast this verse with John 3:8 and Romans 9:19. "The wind bloweth where it listeth, and thou hearest the sound thereof, but canst not tell whence it cometh, and whither it goeth: so is every one that is born of the Spirit" (John 3:8). "Thou wilt say then unto me, Why doth he yet find fault? For who hath resisted his will?" (Rom. 9:19). The latter references refer to regeneration (the internal, subjective, immediate, and efficient work of the Spirit). "The eyes of your understanding being enlightened; that ye may know what is the hope of his calling, and what the riches of the glory of his inheritance in the saints, And what is the exceeding greatness of his power to us-ward who believe, according to the working of his mighty power. Which he wrought in Christ, when he raised him from the dead, and set him at his own right hand in the heavenly places" (Eph. 1:18-20).

12. The will of the sinner, in the first act of conversion, does not move to embrace Jesus Christ except as he moves in the power of the regenerating Spirit. If this is not true, then the act of the sinner turning to God in conversion is nothing more than a natural act. But there is an inward, secret act of the power

of the Holy Spirit effecting in him the will of conversion unto God.

13. The sinner possesses no potential power for good other than the active power of God's Spirit in regeneration. He has no capacity, by nature, for any acts of conversion. No man ever circumcised his own heart. There must be a new heart, new will, new birth, or new creation before repentance and faith.

14. God's power works, in regeneration, not upon the truth but upon the sinner. God cannot make the truth more true. The power comes from neither the word of the gospel, nor the man who preaches it; it comes from the Spirit of God, Whose instrument is the word. "And take the helmet of salvation, and the sword of the Spirit, which is the word of God" (Eph. 6:17). The word, taken abstractly, separated from the Spirit's work on the soil of the human heart, is called "foolishness of preaching" (I Cor. 1:21). "Who hath believed our report? and to whom is the arm of the Lord revealed?" (Is. 53:1). "But if our gospel be hid, it is hid to them that are lost: In whom the god of this world hath blinded the minds of them which believe not, lest the light of the glorious gospel of Christ, who is the image of God, should shine unto them" (II Cor. 4:3,4). The word does not derive its efficacy from human instrumentality by which it is ministered. The false notion of power residing in the minister is so prevalent in professing Christendom today. However, this *treasure* is in earthen vessels (II Cor. 4:7). The excellency of the power is of God, not His ministers. "But we have this treasure in earthern vessels, that the excellency of the power may be of God, and not of us" (II Cor. 4:7). What are ministers? "So then neither is he that planteth any thing, neither he that watereth; but God that giveth the increase" (I Cor. 3:7). We must not understand this absolutely, but in a comparative and relative sense. Ministers are like trumpets which make no sound if breath is not breathed into them.

15. In regeneration, God gives understanding to the mind that has no understanding of spiritual things. "Now we have received, not the spirit of the world, but the spirit which is of God, that we might know the things that are freely given to us of God. Which things also we speak, not in the words which man's

wisdom teacheth, but which the Holy Ghost teacheth: comparing spiritual things with spiritual. But the natural man receiveth not the things of the Spirit of God: for they are foolishness unto him: neither can he know them, because they are spiritually discerned" (I Cor. 2:12-14). Man, therefore, has become like the beasts that perish, which have no understanding (Ps. 49:12,20). Man has not lost, by the fall, his natural intellectual faculty in things natural and civil; but he has lost his ability to understand things that are spiritual. The understanding which God gives is a revelation. "And we know that the Son of God is come, and hath given us an understanding, that we may know him that is true, and we are in him that is true, even in his Son Jesus Christ. This is the true God, and eternal life" (I John 5:20). "And Jesus answered and said unto him, Blessed art thou, Simon Barjona: for flesh and blood hath not revealed it unto thee, but my Father which is in heaven" (Matt. 16:17). This understanding is subjective, enabling the regenerated person to apprehend what is revealed. "And be renewed in the spirit of your mind" (Eph. 4:23). "And have put on the new man, which is renewed in knowledge after the image of him that created him" (Col. 3:10). A light is communicated to the mind of the man quickened by the Spirit. "For God, who commanded the light to shine out of darkness, hath shined in our hearts, to give the light of the knowledge of the glory of God in the face of Jesus Christ" (II Cor. 4:6). This could never be man's act, either in part or whole.

16. Regeneration is a Divine quickening that makes the soul a fit subject for calling, and a proper subject for conversion.

17. Regeneration is the fountain from which a life of holiness is carried on in sanctification and perfected in glorification.

18. Regeneration takes place in the sphere of the subconsciousness of man, i.e., outside of the sphere of conscious attention. The gospel, however, addresses itself to the consciousness of man.

19. In God's light (the light of regeneration) shall the regenerated see light. "For with thee is the fountain of life: in thy light shall we see light" (Ps. 36:9). Only in the light of the Spirit can one see Jesus Christ, the Light of the world.

20. As the child knows nothing of the genesis of his own existence, so the Christian knows nothing of the beginning of his own existence in regeneration. He cannot know it from his own observation.

21. Regeneration is the begetting of the new life. The effectual call is the bringing forth of that life, by Divine summons, into the light of the gospel. If the hearing of the word (call of the gospel) is indispensible to regeneration, then what about babies who die in infancy? As soon as we distinguish quickening from conversion the light enters. There must first be life before there can be any response to living things.

22. There is a great difference in the manner of the Spirit's working before and after regeneration. Before regeneration, He works upon sinners as dead creatures that work not with Him; after regeneration, He works in their souls prompting and assisting them to work. "Likewise the Spirit also helpeth our infirmities: for we know not what we should pray for as we ought: but the Spirit itself maketh intercession for us with groanings which cannot be uttered" (Rom. 8:26). "Wherefore, my beloved, as ye have always obeyed, not as in my presence only, but now much more in my absence, work out your own salvation with fear and trembling. For it is God which worketh in you both to will and to do of his good pleasure" (Phil. 2:12,13). The Spirit's sanctifying influence remains forever in the souls of the regenerate; consolation belongs to their well-being. In regeneration they are positionally fixed; whereas, in sanctification, they may vary in their condition of life. Regeneration assures of heaven; progressive sanctification brings a foretaste of heaven to the regenerated on earth.

23. The whole change in sinful man, from regeneration and its subsequent results—conversion and sanctification, is by the power of God's Spirit. "And what is the exceeding greatness of his power to us-ward who believe, according to the working of his mighty power" (Eph. 1:19). There is no conflict between regeneration by the Spirit and justification through faith, when faith is understood to be the *gift of God.*

24. Regeneration, subjectively considered, is not an act performed by the sinner. Did Lazarus raise himself from the dead? (John 11).

25. Regeneration of the soul does not change the chemistry of the body. It does not cancel the primeval sentence of physical death. The body of the Christian is subject to death because it is a mortal body.

Part II
CONVERSION

INTRODUCTION

The subject in John 3:14-18 is conversion, not regeneration. It may seem to the untutored Christian that conversion is synonymous with regeneration, but the student of Scripture soon learns to distinguish the difference. Regeneration is the sole act of God in the heart of the sinner, and is described in the Bible by such terms as: *new birth* (John 3:3,5); *God's workmanship* (Eph. 2:10); and a *new creature* (II Cor. 5:17). Conversion, however, is the turning of the regenerate by the influence of God's grace.

Christianity involves a change that is compared to birth. When Nicodemus staggered at this teaching, Christ unveiled what makes the new birth possible—the incarnation. But the Lord Jesus did not stop with the incarnation. He also spoke of the end of incarnation —the death of Christ on the cross. In speaking about the subjective work of Christianity, Christ mentioned only the initial act of the new birth. When speaking of the *cause* of the subjective work, the Lord Jesus referred to the objective work of Himself on the cross. Thus, the regenerated person does not rest upon anything *within* himself. He is led by the indwelling Spirit to look *outside* of himself to embrace the objective Christ in a conversion experience.

Christ taught Nicodemus that the new birth is obtained through the sovereign Spirit applying the merit of Christ's death. Then He showed Nicodemus how the knowledge of salvation is attained through faith in the sacrifice of the Lord Jesus. Believers must learn to rest, not on the flesh, but on the risen and glorified Christ. Thus, Christ is viewed not only as the Averter of wrath, but the Object of love and adoration.

CONVERSION IS HISTORICALLY ILLUSTRATED

Our Lord used many illustrations. In John, chapter three, He borrowed one from human life—*birth;* one from nature—the *wind;* and one from the Scriptures—the *serpent of brass.* The illustration of the serpent of brass is taken from Numbers 21. This reference must not be ignored in the study of John 3:14,15. The Christian should never make the mistake of isolating a few verses from the context of Numbers 21. The Lord Jesus, in His discourse with Nicodemus, did not use a conversion experience in the lives of a redeemed people, and apply it as a means of regeneration.

Israel's sin is recorded for the admonition of God's people for all ages. Paul said "Now all these things happened unto them for ensamples (or types) : and they are written for our admonition, upon whom the ends of the world are come" (I Cor. 10:11). Types or institutions are intended to deepen, expand, and ennoble the circle of thoughts and desires of God's people. Thus, Paul appealed to the experience of the fathers.

Israel complained about being brought out of Egypt to die in the wilderness. She also complained about both the bread and water, the two means of her sustenance. This sin of Israel caused God to send fiery serpents among the people; they bit the people and much people of Israel died. The bite of the serpent is the Divine conviction of what the flesh truly is in the very source of its being. Thus, God brought Israel to the place where she would judge the very root of the mischief. Why did God send fiery serpents? The serpent would call to mind what took place in the garden of Eden. There we have the record of the fall of man. The serpent first stung mankind with the fruit of the tree, and it is by the fruit of another tree that man is converted (I Pet. 2:24). Adam's descendants have been so infected with the serpent's venom as to be called "Generation of vipers." Is there any reason why John the Baptist should not have called the unsaved people to whom he preached, "Generation of vipers?" (Matt. 3:7,8).

It is interesting to notice that God did not remove the serpents, but He did give the remedy for their sting. The fulfillment of this is found in Romans 8:3. Sin is not abolished, but it is condemned. That which brought death upon mankind wrought death in mankind (Rom. 5:12). The venom of the serpents would assuredly terminate in death, in spite of man or help by men. We all sinned in Adam, but Adam continues to sin in us. The brazen serpent foreshadowed the lifted up Christ on the cross. The serpent was an emblem and reminder of the curse. On the cross the Lord Jesus was made a curse for His people (Gal. 3:13). Thus, the atonement is the only healing balm. Pennances, moralities, and all other substitutes are vain. The atonement is as descriptive of sin as it is of salvation. The awesomeness of sin was exhibited at the cross. The brazen serpent exactly resembled the fiery serpent in appearance, so Jesus Christ was made in the likeness of sinful flesh (Rom. 8:3). As the serpent was without venom, so Jesus Christ was without sin. The Scriptures everywhere clearly set forth the great truth of Christ's impeccability. The serpent was made of brass, which is typical of judgment. Serpent and brass together portray sin judged. The fiery serpents, that swarmed the camp of Israel, were publicly exhibited by one made of brass which was stingless and dead. Even so, when I look upon Jesus Christ, I see Him enduring sin in all its fierceness and burning pangs; but I also see the ugly reptile of sin publicly exhibited as helpless and dead. Its power over me is broken. The sting is removed from death. The sting of death is sin (I Cor. 15:54-57).

The serpent of brass was the only remedy provided. God's plan was not that some should be saved one way and some another. The Lord Jesus is the only Mediator between God and men. "For there is one God and one mediator between God and men, the man Christ Jesus" (I Tim. 2:5). "Neither is there salvation in any other: for there is none other name under heaven given among men, whereby we must be saved" (Acts 4:12). The serpent was made of brass, an inferior metal. The Lord Jesus was a root out of a dry ground (Is. 53:2). The phrase, "a root out of a dry ground," considered in connection with Isaiah 11:1, shows that it springs up out of the stump of Jesse. Men are represented as turning away, in disappointment, from this tender plant springing out of such unpromising surroundings. This is why some said, ". . . Can there any good thing come out of Nazareth? . . ." (John 1:46). Both the serpent and the cross were prescribed by God; therefore, the cross is the Divinely appointed means of salvation. The Israelites were bitten by a serpent, and by a serpent they were to be healed. Thus, by man (Adam) came sin, and by Man (the God-Man) salvation comes to God's people.

The Lord Jesus is the nearest relative any Christian can have. He suffered *sympathetically with* men in His public ministry, *vicariously for* men in His death, and *substitutionally for* men when He bore the wrath for the elect. The Lord Jesus must be lifted up, sin must be punished, God's righteousness must be upheld, and all its demands met. Jesus Christ alone could and did meet all these demands. A look at the serpent brought physical healing, soon to be interrupted by death. From a look at Christ, exercised by the faculty of faith wrought in the heart at regeneration, flows soul healing unto salvation. The serpent represented the curse which sin entailed; the brass portrayed God's judgment falling on the one made a sin offering. If the Lord Jesus Christ had been a mere creature He would have been consumed, but He was more than a mere creature. He is the eternal Son of God; and, therefore, the infinite Son was not consumed. As the redeemed Israelites were to look upon the serpent of brass for deliverance, so regenerated sinners, by the power of the Holy Spirit, look upon and embrace Jesus Christ for deliverance. Through faith, the power to live is realized; through faith, the regenerated person becomes conscious of justification. This faith is the gift of God (Eph. 2:8). Those who were converted did not look to Moses, their wounds, or the tabernacle. They did not manufacture some cure of their own. They did not minister to others in order to get relief. They did not even fight the serpents. Thus, those who were converted to Christ do not look at some preacher, their wounds, or some particular denomination. They do not manufacture some cure of their own, or minister to others with the idea of getting personal relief. They do not even believe they can destroy sin; but, through faith, which is the gift of God, they embrace Jesus Christ Who has won the victory for them. Thus, those who are converted to Christ say, ". . . greater is he that is in you, than he that is in the world" (I John 4:4).

The incidents recorded in Numbers 21 are great spiritual landmarks. (1) Their conversion resulted from looking at the serpent of brass. They had already been delivered by blood and power (Ex. 12; 14). (2) They turned toward the sunrising. In this we see Israel's pilgrimage. (3) The conflicts, which were the wars of Jehovah, verse 14, reveal their warfare. (4) The song, which came from inward satisfaction (v. 17), manifests the subjective experience of the Holy Spirit expressing Himself in testimony.

Christians must defend themselves but not be agressors when attacked (vs. 33-35). Israel went forward, but they were not yet in the land; wells are found in the wilderness. They were healed, walked, and sang the songs of praise with joy. They met with people with whom they did not wish to have war; but their enemies did not allow them to pass peaceably. Our warfare is with those who oppose our inheritance beyond Jordan. (5) They experienced victory (vs. 21-35). It is a wonderful experience for God's people to possess their possessions.

CONVERSION IS DESCRIBED

A transition from regeneration to conversion is by a special operation of the Holy Spirit; the former issues into the latter. Conversion may be a sharply marked crisis in the life of an individual, but it may also come in the form of a gradual process.

Two words for conversion are employed in the Old Testament. The first serves to express a deep feeling of either sorrow or relief. It is used not only of man but of God. "And it repented the Lord that he had made man on the earth; and it grieved him at his heart. And the Lord said, I will destroy man whom I have created from the face of the earth; both man, and beast, and the creeping thing, and the fowls of the air; for it repenteth me that I have made them" (Gen. 6:6,7). "And the Lord repented of the evil which he thought to do unto his people" (Ex. 32:14). (Judg. 2:18). The second word, which means to turn, turn about, and return, is most commonly used for conversion in the Old Testament. This word is most prominent in the prophets, where it refers to Israel's return to the Lord.

Three words in the New Testament come into consideration in the study of conversion. The one most commonly used refers to the conscious life of man, when his mind is changed. The change indicated by this word has reference to: (1) The intellectual life, "In meekness instructing those that oppose themselves; if God peradventure will give them repentance to the acknowledging of the truth" (II Tim. 2:25). This is identical with the action of faith. (2) The conscious volitional life, a turning from self to God, "Repent therefore of this thy wickedness, and pray God, if perhaps the thought of thine heart may be forgiven thee" (Acts 8:22). (3) The emotional life, "For godly sorrow worketh repentance to salvation not to be repented of: but the sorrow of the world worketh death" (II Cor. 7:10). This change is accompanied with godly sorrow, and opens new fields of enjoyment for the repentant sinner. To be converted is not merely to pass from one conscious direction to another, but to do so with a clearly perceived aversion to the former direction. Conversion, therefore, has not only a positive but a negative side. It looks backward as well as forward. The converted person becomes conscious of his ignorance and error, his wilfulness and folly. "Unto the pure all things are pure: but unto them that are defiled and unbelieving is nothing pure; but even their mind and conscience is defiled" (Titus 1:15). The second word, used in the New Testament, has a somewhat wider signification than the one just used. It really indicates the final act of conversion. "Repent ye therefore, and be converted, that your sins may be blotted out, when the times of refreshing shall come from the presence of the Lord" (Acts 3:19). In this verse, both the first and second words that I have mentioned are used alongside each other. Sometimes the first word contains the idea of repentance only, while the latter always includes the element of faith. The third word, to which I refer, is used only in the verbal form in the New Testament; and literally means to become distressed afterwards. It is found only five times in the New Testament (Matt. 21:29,32; 27:3; II Cor. 7:10; Heb. 7:21). Repentance does not necessarily mean true repentance.

The Bible does not always speak of conversion in the same sense. The nation of Israel repeatedly turned her back on God; and, after experiencing the displeasure of God, repented of her sin and returned unto the Lord. We would call this *national conversion*. Another Biblical example of national conversion is found in Jonah 3. There was an outward reformation of life, among the Ninevites, at the preaching of Jonah.

There are, what can be called, *temporary conversions*. The conversion of individuals, that represents no change of heart, falls into this category. It could not be said that they turned to Jesus Christ. People, who are converted from one false religion to another and not converted to Jesus Christ, have experienced only a temporary conversion. "But he that received the seed into stony places, the same is he that heareth the word, and anon with joy receiveth it; Yet hath he not root in himself, but dureth for a while: for when tribulation or persecution ariseth because of the word, by and by he is offended" (Matt. 13:20,21). (I Tim. 1:19,20; II Tim. 2:17,18; I John 2:19; Heb. 10:38).

There are those who are *truly converted to truth and Jesus Christ*. Examples of such conversion experiences are: Naaman (II Kings 5:5-15), Zacchaeus (Luke 19:8,9), the Samaritan woman (John 4:28,39), the Ethiopian Eunuch (Acts 8:30-39), Saul of Tarsus (Acts 9:5), Cornelius (Acts 10:44), and Lydia, the seller of purple (Acts 16:14).

There are many illustrations of *repeated conversions*, and these only manifest the restoration of God's people (Luke 22:32; Rev.

2:5,16,21,22; 3:3,19). Growth after regeneration is never called a birth, but it issues in many experiences called conversion.

What are some of the characteristics of conversion? Conversion is simply one part of the saving process, but it is a vital part of an organic process. We must show what its position is in this scheme of classification. There is a strong tendency, on the part of most people today, to glorify conversion as if it were the most important part of the saving process. But let me emphasize, *there can never be an act of conversion unless there has already been a previous work of grace,* by the Holy Spirit, in regeneration. Conversion alters, not the position but the *condition* of man.

CONVERSION IS THE CONSEQUENCE OF REGENERATION

The act of God in regeneration is followed by the act of man in conversion. It has been said that the Bible teaches regeneration, but it does not teach re-regeneration. Thus, ". . . He that is washed (had a full bath, which is regeneration) needeth not save to wash his feet, but is clean every whit (as a whole) : and ye are clean, but not all" (John 13:10). God's act in regeneration initiates action in man, which is conversion. *Conversion is a spiritual act, but there can never be a spiritual act apart from spiritual life,* which is wrought in the heart of the sinner in regeneration. Conversion takes place, not in the subconscious but in the conscious life of man. This does not mean that it is not rooted in the subconscious life, but it brings out the close connection between regeneration and conversion. Conversion marks the conscious beginning, not only of the putting away of the old man but also the putting on of the new man. The converted man consciously forsakes the old life and turns to the new life of communion with God through Jesus Christ.

The two words, regeneration and conversion, are used synonymously by some; yet, in most cases they refer to different but closely related matters. Logically, conversion follows regeneration. It should be borne in mind that conversion, which is the activity of man, always results from a previous work of God in man. "Turn thou us unto thee, O Lord, and we shall be turned; renew our days as of old" (Lam. 5:21). "For it is God which worketh in you both to will and to do of his good pleasure" (Phil. 2:13). The fact that man is active in conversion is quite evident from such Scriptures as: Is. 55:7; Jer. 18:11; Ezek. 18:23,32; Acts 2:38; 17:30.

To illustrate that man is not passive in conversion, let us consider Jeremiah 31:18-21: "I have surely heard Ephraim bemoaning himself thus; Thou hast chastised me, and I was chastised, as a bullock unaccustomed to the yoke: turn thou me, and I shall be turned; for thou art the Lord my God. Surely after that I was turned, I repented; and after that I was instructed, I smote upon my thigh: I was ashamed, yea, even confounded, because I did bear the reproach of my youth. Is Ephraim my dear son? is he a pleasant child? for since I spake against him, I do earnestly remember him still: therefore my bowels are troubled for him; I will surely have mercy upon him, saith the Lord. Set thee up waymarks, make thee high heaps: set thine heart toward the highway, even the way which thou wentest: turn again, O virgin of Israel, turn again to these thy cities." According to this passage of Scripture, grace must first enter a man's heart before it can be discovered in his life in conversion. The God of all grace, first of all, draws us, or else we shall never move toward Him.

Quickening grace opens the heart to godly sorrow, and this always issues in evangelical repentance. Repentance is an abiding characteristic or principle of the new heart. The heart is by nature impenitent. It has a natural fitness to sin and is without shame or sorrow. The heart is, by grace, penitent, broken, and contrite. It has a fitness to repent, an aptitude to mourn over sin. This is a permanent principle, or source of sorrow for sin and turning from it to holiness. Repentance is the gift of God. "Him hath God exalted with his right hand to be a Prince and a Saviour, for to give repentance to Israel, and forgiveness of sins" (Acts 5:31). "When they heard these things, they held their peace, and glorified God, saying, Then hath God also to the Gentiles granted repentance unto life" (Acts 11:18). The powerlessness of man is recorded in Jeremiah 31:18,19, ". . . turn thou me and I shall be turned . . . ." The text goes on to speak of the effects of this turning, "Surely after that I was turned, I repented. . . ." The truly saved do not spring in one leap from the rebelliousness of a sinner to the rejoicing of a saint. Instruction and application follow the turning of a repentant sinner. Notice the affect of instruction on Ephraim. He said, "I was ashamed." Repentance, therefore, gives to the mind of the repentant a just sense of his sins and also an appreciation of the redemption and grace in Jesus Christ.

What are the evidences of repentance unto life? We are not forgiven upon repentance because it in any wise compensates, takes away, or diminishes the desert of punishment; but because of the respect that repentance has to compensation already made. All sin is against God. It is infinitely heinous because it is against the infinite God. Sin, therefore, has infinite demerit, and stirs up within the infinite Saviour an infinite indignation for sin. There can be no repentance answerable to the heinous demerit of sin, and there can be no infinite sorrow for infinite sin by the finite sinner. God does not forgive the sinner on the grounds of his finite sorrow;

but on the basis of the infinite punishment of man's infinite sin in the death of the infinite Saviour, and the repentant sinner's respect for that infinite sacrifice. The soul of the repentant man is careful to discriminate between good and evil, light and darkness. His soul struggles against every unholy propensity, every sinful habit. He exercises himself to have a conscience void of offence toward both God and man. This is not a temporary change in his life. His whole course of life is one of repentance and will not be completed until he is made perfect in glory. Every born again person knows that the will to repent is subject to God turning him. God's turning of him is not subject to the will of the sinner to repent.

Conversion is as natural to regenerated man as motion is to a living body. A principle of activity will produce action. Therefore, the principle of grace, wrought in the heart of a sinner in regeneration, produces a condition of life that reflects one's position in Christ.

Divine conviction is a conversion experience. This conversion experience is the fruit of regeneration. It cannot be said, however, that all sinners are completely insensitive to the word of God. It has been suggested that some may be sensible to the evil of sin with regard to themselves, but they do not recognize that their sin is against God. Damnation may scare them, but pollution does not. Hell may frighten them, but offending God does not.

Whatever arises from self always aims at and ends in self. The following are several examples from the Bible to show that all sinners are not completely insensitive to the word of God: (1) Peter speaks of sows which were washed and then returned to wallowing in the mire (II Pet. 2:20-22). (2) Our Lord speaks about the soils which produced stalks but no fruit (Matt. 13). (3) Agrippa said, "Almost thou persuadest me to be a Christian" (Acts 26:28). (4) Ezekiel told about those who come as God's people, sit as they sit, and talk about the message as a lovely song, and yet do nothing about what they hear (Ezek. 33:30-33). (5) There is in unregenerate men a great deal of natural security (Luke 11:21).

THE HOLY SPIRIT IS THE AGENT IN CONVERSION

There is a difference in the working of external providence upon the non-elect and the internal working of the Spirit in the elect who have been regenerated. Peter says that men may know the way of righteousness. "For it had been better for them not to have known the way of righteousness, than, after they have known it, to turn from the holy commandment delivered unto them" (II Pet. 2:21). Luke says they may rejoice in the light of the word for a season. "They on the rock are they, which, when they hear, receive the word with joy; and these have no root, which for a while believe, and in time of temptation fall away" (Luke 8:13). Paul says they may make great sacrifices. "And though I bestow all my goods to feed the poor, and though I give my body to be burned, and have not charity, it profiteth me nothing" (I Cor. 13:3). Matthew says they may perform great works. "Not every one that saith unto me, Lord, Lord, shall enter into the kingdom of heaven; but he that doeth the will of my Father which is in heaven. Many will say to me in that day, Lord, Lord, have we not prophesied in thy name? and in thy name have cast out devils? and in thy name done many wonderful works? And then will I profess unto them, I never knew you: depart from me, ye that work iniquity" (Matt. 7:21-23). Thus, many deeds may be performed and many things may be wrought in the mind, by the dispensation of the gospel, apart from regeneration.

There is a twofold darkness, *objective* and *subjective*. Darkness is a metaphorical expression denoting the natural state of every man. Objective darkness consists of the want of those means whereby men may be enlightened in the knowledge of God (Ps. 19:7-11; 119:105; II Pet. 1:19). Paul was indebted to take the light of the gospel to Rome (Rom. 1:14,15). But the Holy Spirit alone can dispel the darkness of depravity (Acts 16:6-13). Subjective darkness is the darkness of the unregenerate. The light shines in darkness and the darkness comprehends it not (John 1:5). Whatever light men might have by nature, or may gather from the book of creation, will not enable them to comprehend the light of God shining in the face of Jesus Christ (II Cor. 4:6). This subjective darkness can be dispersed only by the work of the Spirit in regeneration. The regenerated person is called out of darkness into light. Paul said, concerning the Ephesians, that they were once darkness but now are light in the Lord (Eph. 5:8). This is not a light produced by the fire of man's own kindling. Men may sit in the presence of the light of the gospel and not know their true condition. "Because thou sayest, I am rich, and increased with goods, and have need of nothing; and knowest not that thou art wretched, and miserable, and poor, and blind, and naked" (Rev. 3:17).

In calling men to the saving knowledge of God and faith in Christ Jesus, the Holy Spirit convinces them of sin, righteousness, and judgment (John 16:11). The Holy Spirit is the great Convincer. Christ said to His disciples, "Nevertheless I tell you the truth; It is expedient for you that I go away: for if I go not away, the Comforter will not come unto you; but if I depart, I will send him unto you" (John 16:7). Our Lord's purpose, on the eve of His departure, was to encourage the disciples. They were saddened by Christ's announcement that He was going back to the Father. During Christ's absence, the disciples were to be engaged in a difficult ministry. They would be hated, opposed, and persecuted. The Lord assured them that the Holy Spirit would comfort, strengthen, and draw the elect of God. How could human sight perceive that it would ever be expedient for the Lord Jesus to depart from the presence of the disciples? We are short sighted and judge by whatever is within range of our vision. The Lord Jesus said that His departure was for their advantage. Let this be a lesson to us that we be not hasty in accepting things at first sight. Let us not say, when perhaps we are on the very road to blessing, all these things are against us. Expediency implies suitability of action to circumstances, of means to accomplish an end, that end being what seemed meet unto Christ. Man recognizes the meaning of the word and thinks he acts upon it; but being evil, he often forgets moral principles. Moreover, he is so ignorant he often chooses wrong means. But with God there are no mistakes. There is absolute righteousness in Him; He does right with the right motive, in the right way, and at the right time. He sees the end from the beginning. All departures are painful and trying; but in the instance of Christ, their Comforter was leaving them. However, He would send them another Comforter. Christ's departure was for the disciples' advantage. The *subjective Spirit* gives a clear understanding of the *objective Christ*. As it was with the disciples, so it is with us today.

Is the conviction of the Spirit to be interpreted as referring to both the elect and the reprobate? If we are to look upon this passage of Scripture in John 16:8-11 as belonging to the elect in the work of their conversion, not regeneration, the words contain the *method* of bringing about this work. *The Holy Spirit is said to accomplish three things*: (1) He *convinces of sin*. How does the Holy Spirit convince of sin? He does so by revealing, to those who possess the Spirit, their depravity. He reveals not only the sins of nature but the nature of sin. The Spirit is the immediate cause of this conviction. Without His immediate influence, we may hear the law preached all our lives and not be once affected by it. "For I was alive without the law once: but when the commandment came, sin revived, and I died. And the commandment, which was ordained to life, I found to be unto death. For sin, taking occasion by the commandment, deceived me, and by it slew me" (Rom. 7:9-11). The Holy Spirit causes the word of God to come to the regenerate person, and the word effectively enters the very center and heart of his life. The one who hears the call of the gospel is often heard to say, "That was preached directly to me." Instead of becoming angry, he feels a deep sense of shame and remorse. Only the Spirit of regeneration can convince. Conscience cannot, public opinion cannot, and the law of Moses can never bring about this Divine conviction. However, the Spirit's application of the word can. (2) *The Holy Spirit convinces of righteousness*. He convinces the recipients of the Spirit, not of their own but of Christ's righteousness. The righteousness of Christ includes both that of His Person and His Work. Notice the order of the Spirit's work. There must be a righteousness, since we are accountable to God Who is righteous. No unclean thing can ever come into heaven; therefore, we must be made righteous in the righteousness of Christ. This righteousness is revealed to the regenerate person by the indwelling Spirit. No one will ever desire righteousness until he is convinced of sin. A man may acknowledge some fruit of sin, while at the same time be completely ignorant of sin's root. The unregenerate person has a false view of righteousness; but the one who has been regenerated embraces the Biblical view of righteousness, which is imputed in justification and imparted in sanctification. (3) *The Holy Spirit convinces of judgment*. He convicts of judgment in relation with the object or things with which it is employed. All judgment is committed to Jesus Christ. The prince of this world has been judged (John 12:31-33). Thus, the regenerated person is convinced that sin is conquered, and it shall finally pass away. The Spirit reveals its overthrow in Christ. It is not enough to be convinced of the righteousness of judgment. Redeemed man knows that the Judge of all the earth will do right (Gen. 18:25). God's judgment is a righteous judgment (Rom. 2:5). It has been said that what blossoms are to fruit, conviction is to conversion. But do not forget, conviction is the fruit of regeneration.

THE HOLY SPIRIT CALLS TO CONVERSION

Calling is the gracious work of the Spirit, whereby He causes the regenerated man to embrace the Lord Jesus freely as He is offered in the gospel (II Thess. 2:14). Calling may be distinguished from regeneration, yet it is closely connected with it. The gracious work of the Holy Spirit in regeneration causes the recipient to respond to the call. The Holy Spirit operates upon man's will, not forcibly bending it but making it pliant and tender from within. Calling addresses itself to the consciousness of man. Thus, regeneration works from within; calling from without. *Calling is the Divine summons, which appeals to the principle of life, that causes the will and understanding to begin to act.* Regeneration and calling differ in this respect: regeneration takes place independently of understanding; while in calling, understanding and will begin to act. Regeneration enables one to hear and understand; thus, with the inclined will he is willing to go out to the light. Regeneration is the begetting of the new life. Calling is the *bringing forth* of that life, by Divine summons, into the light of the gospel. Is not this the order in the following verses? "Who hath saved us, and called us with an holy calling, not according to our works, but according to his own purpose and grace, which was given us in Christ Jesus before the world began, But is now made manifest by the appearing of our Saviour Jesus Christ, who hath abolished death, and hath brought life and immortality to light through the gospel" (II Tim. 1:9,10). "But we are bound to give thanks alway to God for you, brethren beloved of the Lord, because God hath from the beginning chosen you to salvation through sanctification of the Spirit and belief of the truth: Whereunto he called you by our gospel, to the obtaining of the glory of our Lord Jesus Christ" (II Thess. 2:13,14). Does this not prove that regeneration precedes calling? Calling that is effectual presupposes life. What would you think of a woman who said she was going to have a baby when she was not even pregnant? This is a perfect analogy of the person who says that calling precedes regeneration. This calling, therefore, is not a calling of persons who are unregenerate because they have no hearing ear.

The call of the regenerate is something more than the general call, going forth by the preaching of the gospel. While the preaching of the gospel is general to all nations, the content of the preaching is particular. The Bible teaches that men are brought to believe on Jesus Christ; but it is God, not man, Who sends the messengers and determines the recipients. When the gospel is proclaimed to any audience, that audience, from one point of view, is undifferentiated in this respect—all the members of the audience are alike in their depravity. There is no spiritual receptivity. But from another viewpoint, those who hear the word are indeed differentiated, for it is God Who gives the hearing ear (Prov. 20:12). There are many called, that is, by the external preaching of the gospel; but few chosen. And the few chosen are, or shall be, effectually called. "For many are called, but few are chosen" (Matt. 22:14). In this verse, we have two views: the undifferentiated in the first part of the text and the differentiated in the latter part.

In regeneration the sinner is dead to spiritual life. He is absolutely like a corpse, but his first passivity and his subsequent cooperation to the Divine call must not be confounded. Let there be clear insight into this distinction, which is very simple. The elect but unregenerated sinner can do nothing; that which is wrought in him must be by God. This is the first work of grace; but after that is accomplished, the sinner is no longer passive. He is then made active in spiritual things by the power of the new life. This does not mean, however, that the elect and regenerated sinner is able to do anything without God. *All spiritual good from regeneration to glorification is of grace.* He that is called must be able to come; he is made able by regeneration.

The Divine summons is not merely calling a person to tell him something, but it implies the command to come. There is something determinate about the effectual call. Thus, Paul said, ". . . called according to his purpose" (Rom. 8:28). A summons issued by a court does not of itself empower us to appear in court. Our appearance there depends on our strength and will. It might become necessary for an officer of the court to apprehend and compel us to appear because we lack the will to appear. But the elect sinner has already been apprehended by regeneration before the call comes to him (Matt. 22:1-14; Luke 14:15-24; Phil. 3:12,13). Does not regeneration affect the will? God's people are willing in the day of His power (Ps. 110:3). The effectual call is from darkness to light (I Pet. 2:9). When an individual is converted, regeneration and calling seem to coincide; they do to his consciousness, but they are distinct. They differ in this respect: regeneration is wrought in one without his cooperation; calling includes his cooperation.

In calling, the will and understanding begin to act so that we hear with both the outward and inward ear; and with the inclined will, we are willing to go out to the light. As there is time between implanting seed in the womb and bringing forth a child in birth, so is it in the spiritual realm with this important difference—no one knows when the work of regeneration takes place. With John the Baptist, it was before his birth. He was still in his mother's womb (Luke 1:41-45; Jer. 1:5; Gal. 1:15,16). God's calling does not have its starting point in the preacher. He that calls is God, not the minister (Rom. 8:28). This calling is heavenly (Heb. 3:1), holy (II Tim. 1:9), high in Christ Jesus our Lord (Phil. 3:14), and according to God's purpose (Rom 8:28). Though the call does not begin with the preacher, yet it includes him.

The call of the regenerate is twofold: from without, by the preaching of the word; but from within, by exhortation and conviction of the Holy Spirit. Hence, the call by the Holy Spirit is twofold: (1) He uses the word, which is inspired, prepared, committed to writing, preserved, and proclaimed by the Spirit called minister; (2) He illuminates the understanding to recognize and respond to the call. Understanding results in Divine conviction. His calling is without repentance (Rom. 11:29). This is a bridge which can be crossed but once. Once it is crossed there is no going back. It is unchangeable, irreversible, and irrevocable. The appeal is to the faithfulness of God. Calling without repentance, refers not to man but God. God does not change His purpose. Thus, calling has its foundation in election and its end in glorification. It is from God's purpose (Rom. 8:28), to His eternal glory (I Pet. 5:10).

Believers are exhorted to make their calling sure (II Pet. 1:10). Through making our calling sure, we make our election sure—sure to ourselves. Observe the order, (1) Calling, then (2) Election. Only through calling can we make election sure. Calling is used here in the sense of result or evidence of election. Calling is confirmed by a holy life. There is no firmness in hypocrites.

The effectual call is personal, not general. Zacchaeus made haste and came down when he was called (Luke 19:5). God's grace and call humble. Christ said, "I must." There is no standing against it. You will notice that the Lord invited Himself; Zacchaeus did not invite Christ (Luke 19:5). The Lord Jesus not only invited Himself, but He said, "I must abide at thy house." When the Lord says *must*, it must be. This call was effectual because Zacchaeus embraced Christ and produced good works. "For this cause also thank we God without ceasing, because, when ye received the word of God which ye heard of us, ye recieved it not as the word of men, but as it is in truth, the word of God, which effectually worketh also in you that believe" (I Thess. 2:13). The sheep of Christ hear His voice and follow Him (John 10). Though we often complain that it is hard to get people to listen to the gospel, let us never forget that Jesus Christ said, "My sheep hear my voice." The effectual call gives God His rightful place as the prime Mover in the work of grace.

Calling is entirely on the Divine side (Rom. 8:30). The *effect* of God's call is that *Jesus Christ becomes a personal reality* to everyone who is called. The most wonderful preaching in the world cannot produce that. There is only one test which can show whether we are right or wrong. It is our attitude toward Jesus Christ. The call of God brings about something in the regenerated soul that must work its way out. No natural hindrance can stand in its way. The Divine call separates a person from all man-made schemes for putting things right. Hence, the person who has been effectually called of God cannot deny that Jesus Christ is in him. Saints have been called of Jesus Christ (Rom. 1:6); this denotes privilege. They are called saints (Rom. 1:7); this speaks of position. They are called according to God's eternal purpose, and this refers to God's plan (Rom. 8:28). They are called children of the living God, which refers to their perpetuity (Rom. 9:26).

MEANS ARE USED IN CONVERSION

Ministers are used as instruments in converting people, but not in regenerating them. It is striking to observe that in three New Testament passages, where conversion is used transitively of converting someone to God, the subject of the verb is not God but a preacher. "And many of the children of Israel shall he turn to the Lord their God" (Luke 1:16). "Delivering thee from the people, and from the Gentiles, unto whom now I send thee, To open their eyes, and to turn them from darkness to light, and from the power of Satan unto God, that they may receive forgiveness of sins, and inheritance among them which are sanctified by faith that is in me" (Acts 26:17,18). "Brethren, if any of you do err from the truth, and one convert him; Let him know, that he which converteth the sinner from the error of his way, shall save a soul from death, and shall hide a multitude of sins" (Jas. 5:19,20). The conversion of men is to be the objective of ministers and churches, but we cannot be instruments of conversion in people where there has been no work of God in regeneration. Therefore, our first plea is for the power of God in regeneration, and then for men to repent and believe. ". . . Be ye reconciled to God" (II Cor. 5:19,20); receive reconciliation (Rom. 5:10,11).

Let me emphasize the fact that external preaching of the word *alone* does not effect conviction that is of God. Conviction that is of God is the fruit of regeneration (John 16:8-11). Pretended believers may have their natural faculties illuminated to the extent that the seed of the word brings some visible growth, but they are rocky and thorny ground hearers (Matt. 13; Luke 8). Any conviction that comes from the mere preaching of the word is no more than moral suasion. Apart from the work of the Spirit within the heart, there will be no lasting effect of external preaching. The internal Spirit of life is required to apply the external word. The regenerated person realizes, by the indwelling Spirit, that this word comes to him directly from God. It affects and condemns his very being; thus, it causes him to penetrate into the hidden essence of the word and feel the sharp sting which effects Divine conviction. Divine conviction is related to and is inseparable from regeneration.

We have confirmed the fact that Divine conviction is the fruit of the indwelling Spirit, wrought in the heart in regeneration. We shall now show that this conviction is produced by the gospel. It is not a question of whether God works regeneration by means of a creative word or command. One must admit that He does, in the light of the two following verses. "And God said, Let there be light: and there was light" (Gen. 1:3). "And when I passed by thee, and saw thee polluted in thine own blood, I said unto thee when thou wast in thy blood, Live; yea, I said unto thee when thou wast in thy blood, Live" (Ezek. 16:6). The real question is whether God, in regenerating the new life, employs the word of preaching as an instrument or means.

We must never forget that regeneration takes place immediately in the sphere of the subconsciousness, while the truth of the gospel addresses itself to the consciousness of man. Thus, the truth of the gospel can exercise its persuasive influence only when man's attention is fixed upon it. In order for man's attention to be fixed upon the gospel, there must first be a work of grace in his heart. This is the work of regeneration. It is vain to talk of the persuasive power of the truth of the gospel regenerating men. We know that both the sun and rain may shed their influences on the desert, and yet the desert remains a desert. When, however, those influences fall on a fertile field, it is clothed with the wonders of vegetable fertility and beauty. We are also cognizant of the fact that the midday brightness of the sun has no more affect on the eyes of a blind man than a candle. It is so with the truth of the gospel upon a person whose heart has not been touched by grace in regeneration.

No matter what the inherent power is of the gospel, it fails of any spiritual effect, unless the mind to which it is presented is in a fit state to receive it. "But the natural man receiveth not the things of the Spirit of God: for they are foolishness unto him: neither can he know them, because they are spiritually discerned" (I Cor. 2:14). The Lord Jesus said to the Jews, "Why do ye not understand by speech? even because ye cannot hear my word" (John 8:43). (John 8:47). Experience confirms this teaching of the Bible. Is not the word quick and powerful? Yes, but the Bible also says that Christ gave the apostles power to work miracles; the power, however, was not in the apostles (Acts 3:12; 10:25,26).

Without the objective truth, concerning the work of Jesus Christ, every regenerated soul would remain in darkness, as an unborn infant in relation to the external world. The Bible distinguishes the influence of the Holy Spirit from that of the word of the gospel. It declares that such an influence is necessary for the proper reception of truth (John 6:64,65; Acts 16:14; I Cor. 2:12-15; Eph. 1:17-20). Notice particularly the instance of Lydia in Acts 16: she ". . . heard us: whose heart the Lord opened, that she attended unto the things which were spoken of Paul." There is no more disposition in unregenerate men to receive the gospel of Christ than there is in darkness to receive light, the dead to receive life, or the deaf to hear. The mind of unregenerate man remains a responsible subject to embrace the gospel; but he has no active power or disposition toward it, until there has been a work of grace in his heart.

The question is often asked, does regeneration precede, accompany, or follow the hearing of the gospel? In order to answer this question correctly, one must consider what is meant by the word *hearing*. Is this the ear that hears or the organ of the human body called ear? To be technical, the Holy Spirit may perform His work of regeneration before, during, or after the external call of the gospel. If I were to designate the whole conscious work of grace from conversion until death, without any regard to regeneration's mysterious origin, then I must use the word of the gospel as an instrument. However, if I distinguish, in this work of grace, between the origin of the new life and its support, then regeneration ceases immediately after man is born again. We must distinguish between the conscious and unconscious work of God.

The word of the gospel is to effect conversion and practical sanctification, not regeneration. It is argued by some that the life is in the seed of the gospel and comes forth out of the seed, but this will not stand the test of Scripture. It is not Biblical to state that the Spirit, or principle of life, is shut up in the word, just as the living germ is enclosed in the seed. Our Saviour, in the parable of the sower (Matt. 13:1-9), was explaining how the seed of the word bears fruit in some cases, and not in others. Only the prepared soil, which represents regeneration, understands and brings forth fruit.

GOD'S LOVE IS THE CAUSE OF CONVERSION

We now approach the most quoted, but most misunderstood verse in the whole Bible. The text is John 3:16. The love of God, that we hear so much about today, is according to a definite plan. It is not love in general, but love in a particular, personal sense. Thus, it is *not indiscriminate*. God's love and attention are explained and limited in John 3:16. The person who emphasizes man's free will charges God with two contrary ends and designs at the same time: (1) He accuses God of condemning many whom He sent His Son not to condemn, but to save; and (2) he charges God with loving many upon whom His wrath shall always abide. The Lord Jesus took care to explain the Father's intention in John 3:14,15. There is nothing stated to indicate that God loves every man, or that the Son came to redeem every man. The Lord Jesus gave His flesh for the life of the world (John 6:51), but the Scripture nowhere states that He gave His flesh for every man. He is the propitiation for the sins of the whole world, but He is not the propitiation for every man (I John 2:2). Paul said, "Whom God hath set forth to be a propitiation through faith in his blood, to declare his righteousness for the remission of sins that are past, through the forebearance of God" (Rom. 3:25). According to this verse, Jesus Christ is not a propitiation to those who have no faith. Those who emphasize free will can plead only one word in John 3:16, and that word is *world*. They do not recognize that the word *world* is used many ways in Scripture. This shall be explained in our exposition of this text.

Paul, in writing to the Colossians, said: ". . . the gospel; which is come unto you, as it is in all the world; and bringeth forth fruit . . ." (Col. 1:5,6). But the question is, does the gospel bring forth fruit in unbelievers? The Scriptures state that, ". . . all the world should be taxed" (Luke 2:1); ". . . all the world wondered after the beast" (Rev. 13:3); ". . . Satan . . . deceiveth the whole world . . ." (Rev. 12:9); ". . . the whole world lieth in wickedness" (I John 5:19). Thus, the word *kosmos*, translated world in our King James version, is used of the universe (Acts 17:24); the earth (John 13:1); humanity minus believers (John 15:18; Rom. 3:6; II Pet. 2:5); Gentiles in contrast to Jews (Rom. 11:12); and believers only (John 6:33; 12:47; II Cor. 5:19). The reference to the word *world* in Luke 2:1 refers to the Roman world.

"The whole world" in Romans 1:8 refers to the saints. In Revelation 13:3, ". . . the world wondered after the beast," yet we know there were some who did not receive his mark; so they did not wonder after him. The elect cannot be deceived (Rev. 12:9); so the statement, ". . . the whole world lieth in wickedness" (I John 5:19), does not refer to the saved because they do not belong to the world. The saved are in it, but not of it (John 17:14).

The word *whosoever* in John 3:16 is the world-wide application of God's purpose. Thus, salvation is not confined to one particular nation or rank. *Whosoever* refers to the *Gentiles* as well as the *Jews*. Someone might raise the question: Do you not believe in whosoever will? Yes, I do. But the question is, who can will? The will that is to determine is the same will that is to be, and must be determined by grace. The disease, therefore, is in the will. How can a diseased will provide the cure for a depraved soul? The great truth announced here, to a religious Jew, shows him that the Gentile is included in God's love and that the Jews are not the exclusive objects of His affections. The *world* in John 3:16,17 must be understood to consist of only the *elect Jews and Gentiles*, for whose salvation and deliverance from condemnation Christ came into the world. If Jesus Christ procured, through His death, a possibility of salvation, He only removed the insuperable obstruction that man might become his own saviour. That would exalt the goodness and power of the creature, and not the merit and grace of God. Did the Lord Jesus only make salvation possible by His death, and man may make his damnation certain by his unbelief? If the Lord Jesus failed in His purpose, why was He exalted to give repentance and remission of sins? (Acts 5:31). What sense can there be in interpreting the word *world* to mean every individual, when God purposes that none but believers shall benefit from His love? This verse begins in eternity with God and ends with man in eternity. The love of God comes, in time, to ransom a host of believing souls.

If the eternality of God is understood, one will have no difficulty interpreting John 3:16. Duration of Divine existence is from eternity, according to our finite way of understanding eternity. Divine duration must be considered as wholly permanent, and the ever present *now*, not capable of division into parts any more than the Divine existence itself. Thus, things future to us are present with God. With this fact properly understood we know that the eternal *God coexists with faith, but faith does not coexist with God.* Because of this eternal fact, Jeremiah said, "The Lord hath appeared of old unto me, saying, Yea, I have loved thee with an everlasting love: therefore with lovingkindness have I drawn thee" (Jer. 31:3).

God's love is uninfluenced. "For when we were yet without strength, in due time Christ died for the ungodly. For scarcely for a righteous man will one die: yet peradventure for a good man some would even dare to die. But God commendeth his love toward us, in that, while we were yet sinners, Christ died for us" (Rom. 5:6-8). Human love is reciprocal. We love because we are loved. *Divine love,* however, *is not a response* to something outside of itself. God loves because that is His nature. Love is God's character, not His characteristic (I John 3:16).

God's love is infinite. The question is raised, is it possible to know the unknowable? Paul's answer is in the affirmative. "And to know the love of Christ, which passeth knowledge, that ye might be filled with all the fulness of God" (Eph. 3:19). The love of God is an intriguing subject. It attracts attention by arousing one's curiosity. God's love is a subject with many sources of reflection, but Paul speaks of only one—its incomprehensibility, "It passeth knowledge." Whatever others may think of themselves, a person who has been born of the Spirit of God readily admits he has done nothing to commend himself to God. People who try to convince us that they have been unfortunate rather than criminal are not manifesting the fruit of grace. That is not a true confession of depravity. Can we really know that which is unknowable? We can know by grace what we cannot know by nature. We can know by faith what we cannot know by reason. We can know the effects without comprehending the cause. We can know the reality of God's existence without understanding the nature of His existence. We may know that increasingly which cannot be known perfectly. "But the path of the just is as the shining light, that shineth more and more unto the perfect day" (Prov. 4:18).

The wisdom of God's people increases. Our ideas of love may be more clear and consistent in the future than they are at the present. We see so dimly now that our eyes are only half open, and too often, confusion seems to reign in many Christian conceptions. Therefore, our hearts need to be established. It is to be lamented that our ideals exceed our actions. Is there not a difference in a principle slumbering in the head and being alive in the heart? Paul's prayer for the Ephesians was that they might be filled with all the fulness of God (Eph. 3:19). Man in his natural condition is empty of God. Man in his glorified state will be full of God— He is all in all. However, man in his gracious state (state of grace) has a degree of both his original emptiness and his final fulness. He is not what he was, neither is he what he will be. He is thankful for what he has, but he wants more of the presence and image of Jesus Christ. Love, therefore, constrains to a life of holiness and service.

God's love is immutable (Jas. 1:17). God does not love all men in the provision of salvation, and hate those who reject it. As we have already stated, God's love is eternal. Since it had no beginning, it can have no ending.

God's love is holy; His love is not regulated by passion or sentiment, but by principle. It never conflicts with His holiness, and will never wink at sin. The highest manifestation of God's love is the Cross.

The source of love is God Himself. The principle object of the love of God is Himself. Self love is in all intelligent beings, and it is not condemned when it is carried on in its proper channel. Persons are not obligated to love others more than themselves, but as themselves (Matt. 22:39). God, therefore, first and chiefly loves Himself. Thus, He has made His glory the chief end of all His works in nature, providence, and grace (Prov. 16.4; Rom. 11:36; Rev. 4:11; Eph. 1:6). The three Divine Persons in the Godhead mutually love each other (John 3:35; 17:24; I Cor. 2:10-12; John 16:14). God is the fountain from Whom love proceeds.

Next in the attributes, which belong to God as a holy and intelligent Spirit, we may consider those which may be called affections. There are some things done by Him which are similar to affections in intelligent beings. They are ascribed to Him as love, hatred, anger, etc. From these, everything which is carnal, sensual, or has any degree of imperfection in it must be removed. Here, love stands first in the affections because God is love, but love is not God's chief attribute. Both *holiness and justice precede love in the Divine order*. God is so holy that He cannot look upon sin (Hab. 1:13). Justice protects His holiness. God's justice must be satisfied in order for holiness to manifest love to the sinner.

God's love has a specific object, the world. The statement "love is of God" does not mean that it comes from God in the same way that light comes from God. It is not asserted of love as it is of light; "And God said, let there be light: and there was light" (Gen. 1:3). He does not say, "Let there be love and there was love." God's love does not shine upon the whole world (all people without exception) as the light of nature does. This love of God is a saving love, not a love which merely tends toward salvation. *God gave* expresses absolute freeness of the gift. *Giving and receiving are relative terms,* the one presupposes the other. God never gives something that is not received. The gift, however, is not to every man; for to whomever He gives His Son He gives all things freely with Him (Rom. 8:32). Since love is God's gift, whoever God loves receives His gift. The world which Jesus Christ came to save is not completed. This is the reason God is long-suffering (II Pet. 3:9). There is no marvel so great, no mystery so unfathomable as this—that the great and good God, whose perfect righteousness flames in indignation at the sight of every iniquity and Whose absolute holiness recoils in the presence of every impurity, loves this sinful world and has so loved it that He gave His only begotten Son to die for it.

John is teaching the *universalism* of Christianity, in contrast with the *nationalism* of the Old Testament. Especially in this universalistic and anti-Jewish gospel of John, what is more natural than to find the *world* brought into contrast with Jewish exclusiveism? He did not come to make propitiation for the Jews only. The elect of God are not the residual of the great conflagration. They are not, so to speak, the ashes of the burned up world gathered sadly together by the Creator after the catastrophe is over, that He may make a new and perhaps better beginning with them, and perchance build from them a new structure to replace that which has been lost. The elect themselves are not the world, as it is in its sin lying in the evil one, but the world with its promise of renewed life. God attaches to Himself, in every generation, those who become His by regeneration. They are no longer a part of the world that lies in the evil one, but a portion of the *regenerated world* that abides in Him. When the process of salvation is completed, then the task which the Son of Man took upon Himself shall also be completed; and the world shall be saved. The wicked world of sinful men will be transformed into a world of righteousness. The statement, *the world shall be saved through*

Christ is a conception independent of the idea that every individual shall be saved through Him. The apostle John did not argue a propitiation for every individual person; but for a propitiation in intention and design, which shall effect a renewal so vast as to issue in an ordered cosmos (world), the "new heavens and the new earth." John 3:16 is a vision of the consummated purpose of the immeasurable love of God. It is a vision of the saved world.

There is strong objection, by those who emphasize *free will*, to what I have given on John 3:16. Their cry is, "Such teaching limits the atonement." I must remind you that every religionist limits the atonement. Those who believe in *free will* limit the *quality* of the atonement, and those who believe in *free grace* limit its *extent*. According to God's word, I would much rather be accused of limiting the extent rather than the quality of redemption. One has said, "The things which we have to choose between are an atonement of high value, or an atonement of wide extension. The two cannot go together."

I must remind you that the value of Christ's atonement was infinite. Just as it is necessary for the sun to give off as much heat for only one plant to grow upon the earth as if the whole world is to be covered with vegetation; so it was necessary for Christ Jesus to suffer as much for the salvation of one soul, as if all mankind were to be saved. If redemption is made universal, its inherent value is destroyed. If it is applied to all men alike and some are lost, the conclusion is that it makes salvation objectively possible for all, but it does not subjectively save anyone. If the benefits of the atonement are universal and unlimited, then the benefit of the sacrifice was to blot out the curse which rested upon the race through the fall, and not a perfect satisfaction which fulfills the demands of Divine justice.

Before leaving John 3:16, I would like to ask five questions, and then seek to give the Biblical answers. I will relate the answers the Bible teaches to each question, after stating what those who believe in free will have to say.

1. What is that love which was the cause of the Father sending the Son into the world?

   Those who believe in *free will* say, "It was a natural propensity to the good of all mankind."

   Those of us who believe in *free grace* say, "Love is not an inclination of God's nature, but an act of His Divine will." There was no imperfection in God's love. A natural affection for all, and not completed and perfected in all, is imperfect and weak. This could never be attributed to the all-sufficient God.

2. Who are the objects of God's love?

Those who believe in *free will* say, "Christ is offered to all men without exception."

Those of us who believe in *free grace* say, "God's love intended the salvation of some." If the word *world* means every person without exception, then His love was defeated because it was not made effectual in all.

4. Who are the "whosoever"?

Those who believe in *free will* say, "It refers to every individual in the world, and can never be restricted in intention to some."

Those of us who believe in *free grace* say, "This love is restricted to believers." Love is an unchangeable intention of the sovereign God.

5. What is the fruit of this love?

Those who believe in *free will* say, "Eternal life is the fruit obtained by faith; but this was not the end intended by God, because He loved and died for all mankind, and many hate and do reject Him."

All who believe in *free grace* say, "The love of God is not in vain." The general ransom is an empty sound because Jesus Christ did not die in vain. Isaiah said, concerning the Lord Jesus, "He shall see His seed and be satisfied." He shall be satisfied with the accomplishment of His intention.

The channel of God's eternal love is the eternal Son. It has been said that love may be where there is no office, and so no power to do us good; but in Jesus Christ love and office meet. They are combined in the Lord Jesus Christ to do good for those whom the Father gave Him. The love of Jesus Christ was the sole compelling cause of His assumption of the office of Mediator (Gal. 2:20; Rev. 1:5). The eternal disposing cause of the whole work, wherein the Lord Jesus was engaged for the redemption and salvation of His people, is the eternal love of God the Father. This love of the Father acted in His eternal decree "before the foundation of the world" (Eph. 1:4), and was afterward manifested in sending His Son to render it effectual (John 3:16).

All who believe Christ's Divine Person profess the valuation of the love of the Son. John said, "Hereby perceive we the love, of God, because he laid down his life for us: and we ought to lay down our lives for the brethren" (I John 3:16). It was wrath, not love, that all mankind deserved. This is a consideration suited to fill the souls of men with self abasement. Jesus Christ is glorious in this love. No creature, angel, or man could have the least conception of it before its effects are manifested. Even after its manifestation in the death of Jesus Christ, it is absolutely incomprehensible in this world (Eph. 3:19). An unseen glory accompanied the Lord Jesus Christ in all that He did during His personal ministry, and in what He suffered when He died on the cross. His glory was unseen by the eyes of the world in general, but not by His own sheep, whom He came to save. If men in general had seen it, they would not have crucified the Lord of glory, according to I Corinthians 2:8.

Did God simply open up a way of salvation through Jesus Christ? Could sinners only walk in a way that was opened to them? Such a meager provision would be operative in no case. The fact that everyone that doeth evil hateth the light and cometh not unto the light is proved by the context of John 3:19,20. How can a way, that has been simply opened, do anything for men who will not come to the light because they hate it? All unbelievers do really in their hearts call Jesus Christ "Ichabod," which means "where is the glory" (I Sam. 4:21). They see neither form nor comliness in him that He should be desired (Is. 53:2). It is true that many do not call Jesus Christ anathema, but they cry, "Hail master" and then crucify Him (Matt. 26:49).

To teach that Jesus Christ only opened a way of salvation leads to a deistic soteriology. What is meant by deistic soteriology? It is the concept that God has done all that He can do, and now the rest is left up to the sinner. *The love of God is a saving love, not a love which merely tends toward salvation.* The almighty, all conquering love of God, therefore, does not pour itself equally and with the same intent upon every man in the world. In the sovereignty, that necessarily belongs to His love, He visits whom He will with it. Thus, the Father is giving, in time, His only begotten Son to those whom He gave to the Son in the convenant of redemption in eternity. The Son of God, by the Holy Spirit, is now giving eternal life to all the Father gave Him. "And this is life eternal, that they might know thee the only true God, and Jesus Christ, whom thou hast sent" (John 17:3).

FAITH IS EXERCISED IN CONVERSION

Before we conclude our study of Regeneration and Conversion from John 3:1-18, I want to emphasize two great truths in the light of verses 17 and 18: (1) the purpose of Christ's first advent (v. 17), and (2) the faith of those whom God ordained to believe (v. 18). The purpose of Christ's first advent was not to judge, but to save those whom the Father gave Him in the covenant of redemption. "As thou hast given him power over all flesh, that he should give eternal life to as many as thou hast given him. And this is life eternal, that they might know thee the only true God, and Jesus Christ, whom thou hast sent" (John 17:2,3).

Those who believe and emphasize free will say, "Christ came that the world of lost sinners might be saved, not saying that it shall be saved. 'Might' expresses a possibility while 'shall' speaks of certainty. If the world for which Christ died is the so-called elect only, then the elect might be saved—not shall be saved. This would indicate that the elect might not be saved, hence eventually lost in hell." The word *might,* in John 3:17, when used relatively denotes inherent ability; and when used absolutely denotes power to carry something into effect. Does the Lord leave any room for doubt about the Scripture being fulfilled in the following verses? "Now all this was done, that it might be fulfilled which was spoken of the Lord by the prophet" (Matt. 1:22). "That it might be fulfilled which was spoken by Esaias the prophet" (Matt. 4:14). Is there any possibility of Christ failing to give life to those whom the Father gave Him? "The thief cometh not, but for to steal, and to kill, and to destroy: I am come that they might have life, and that they might have it more abundantly" (John 10:10). Is there any possibility of Christ failing in His resurrection? "Therefore doth my Father love me, because I lay down my life, that I might take it again" (John 10:17). Is there any possibility of Christ failing to be glorified? ". . . This sickness is not unto death, but for the glory of God, that the Son of God might be glorified thereby" (John 11:4). (John 17:1-24). There is *no uncertainty* of God's purpose for Christ being fulfilled. "For Christ also hath once suffered for sins, the just for the unjust, that he might bring us to God, being put to death in the flesh, but quickened by the Spirit" (I Pet. 3:18). Christ said, "All that the Father giveth me shall come to me; and him that cometh to me I will in no wise cast out" (John 6:37).

Can a person give himself to Jesus Christ to be saved? According to God's word, the answer is, no. Then we must conclude that the person given to Jesus Christ by the Father to be redeemed *shall* be redeemed. Faith in Jesus Christ is the fruit of God's ordination. ". . . as many as were ordained to eternal life believed" (Acts 13:48). True faith, therefore, is the faith of God's elect (Titus 1:1). The record states that all that the Father gave to the Son shall come to the Son, not "if they will come." This promise is so related to the Divine purpose that it cannot fail (Is. 46:11). Hence, *coming* finds its cause in being *given* and *drawn* (John 6:37,44).

The word *world* in John 3:16,17 must be understood to refer to the elect of both Jews and Gentiles, for whose salvation Christ came into the world. The Lord Jesus came into the world to save His own, yet He actually saves only those to whom He gives faith. There is so much talk today about man's free will; thus, many proclaim free will as though it alone had escaped the damage of the fall, and as if Adam had not sinned in that virgin faculty. What an idol Arminians make of free will! The Arminian argument on John 5:40, "Ye will not come to me, that ye might have life," is as follows: (1) Man has a will; (2) He is entirely free; (3) Men must make themselves willing to come to Christ; otherwise, they will not be saved. This argument may sound plausible to the person who has a limited knowledge of the Bible; but in the light of the revelation of God's mind, I present four unanswerable arguments: (1) Every man outside of Jesus Christ is spiritually dead; therefore, he will not come to Christ that he might have *life*. (2) There is life in the Lord Jesus, but John 5:40 states, "Ye will not come to *me*." (3) There is life for everyone that comes to Christ for it, but the text says, "Ye will not come." (4) No man by nature ever will come to Christ (John 6:44). No man can come. Therefore, the sinner, apart from Divine help, is unable to will and unwilling to be able to come to Jesus Christ. According to the context in John 3:16-21, there are *two* different *worlds* and *two* different *loves;* one is from above and the other from beneath. There is, first of all, the world that God so loved that He gave His only begotten Son. And second, there is the world which lies in darkness (I John 5:19). This world loves darkness rather than light (John 3:19,20). Thus, the world outside of Christ lies in darkness and is void of spiritual light and life.

What is meant by the expression, *freedom of the will?* The dictionary states, "The faculty of conscious and particularly of deliberate action; the power of control the mind has over its own actions—the freedom of the will. The power of choosing one's own actions; the act or process of choosing or asserting one's choice; volition—my hands are obedient to my will." Freedom therefore means, "The state of being at liberty rather than being in confinement or under restraint—exemption from external control, interference, or regulation. Free will means the doctrine that human action expresses personal choice and is not solely determined by physical or divine forces—made or done freely or of one's own accord, voluntary."

Let me raise some important questions. (1) Does freedom mean that man is a self-sufficient being? Paul said, ". . . our sufficiency is of God" (II Cor. 3:5). (2) Is there a self-determining factor in the will of man? Arminians call this factor the freedom of the will. If the will determines itself, then the action is both cause and effect. How can it be both? *Every effect has a cause,* and as you go back you must stop with an uncaused cause. An uncaused cause is, by necessity, self-existent and must be eternal and unchangeable. No act of the will can come into existence without a cause, which supposes every act of the will determined with some act of the will going before it. (3) Is the will inclined to do something before it exerts its own power on itself? If this were true, then the inclination is not wholly of itself. It is absurd to suppose that man can have an inclination to something good which is contrary to his nature. Man by nature is sinful; therefore, he does not have any inclination toward that which is good in a spiritual sense. (4) Does liberty consist in the will determining its own acts? If this is true, then the will makes a choice prior to understanding. There can be no act of the will without some motive of inducement. If the will is not determined by some outside power then it seeks, desires, and chooses nothing. Hence, there is no act of choice in this case, and that is to say there is no act of the will. (5) Is man free or is he enslaved? Slavery of fallen man is the only Biblical approach to the subject. Failure to see the proper approach is the root cause of the problem. Man by nature is enslaved to sin and can be made free only by the grace of the sovereign God in regeneration.

Freedom, in the study of Theology, does not refer to a self-sufficient being, but rather, to the *freedom of the man of God*. The will that determines is the will that needs to be determined. Therefore, if the will is determined there must be a determiner. Who is the determiner? The student of Scripture knows that inward actions are above the sinner's ability to direct toward a good cause because the fountain is bad, the tree is corrupt, the mind is darkened, the heart is deceived, and he loves darkness rather than light. If it were possible for the depraved will to be convinced with Divine truth, then it would hate error, not truth. The common view of liberty is that man does as he pleases, but that is inconsistent with liberty. This would make fallen man embrace the very thing that he will not permit God to possess. According to this view, God has no virtue at all. He is deserving of no commendation or praise because He is under necessity. This is blasphemy! God is the highest of all; His virtue is not rewardable. He is infinitely above receiving any reward from the creature and is eternally happy and free. His creatures, therefore, cannot be profitable to Him. God does not live for His creatures but for Himself. If this is not true, then for what did He live before He created? Has He changed? For whom will He live after the present dispensation is finished? Once a person grants that the greater is to be subordinated to the lesser, he is on the road to disaster. This is the evil doctrine of all vain and conceited philosophers.

Man's sin is not a manifestation of his freedom, but of his perversion. Man, who is enslaved to sin, can be made free only by the grace of the sovereign God. The Scriptural witness on freedom is limited to man's relation to God (John 8:32,36). *Freedom*, therefore, *becomes actualized in submission*. The more communion with God, the more free the lives of God's people become. Christians are free from something lesser to something greater.

All who embrace the Lord Jesus Christ by faith (John 3:18) are ordained of God to eternal life (Acts 13:48). What is saving faith? Who shall adequately define faith? Considered in its psychological aspects, it is just about as complicated a subject as one could study. This, however, need not deter us in the least because we are not concerned with faith from the standpoint of psychology. After all, faith can be known only by what it does. Its nature is known by the way it expresses itself. Let me, first of all, clear the ground by answering negatively that faith, which saves the soul, is no mere unreasoning assumption such as often passes for Christian faith. For instance, day after day we hear people chant the words, "I believe," who no more know what it is to believe to the saving of the soul than a pig knows what it is to fly. These people can given no coherent account of what they believe, or why they believe it. Yet, they pass as Christians and actually think within themselves that they are Christians. George Whitfield once asked a man of this sort, "What do you believe?" and the man replied, "I believe what the church believes." Mr. Whitfield then asked, "And what does the church believe?" To which the man replied, O the church believes what I believe," Mr. Whitfield then asked, "What then do you both believe?" The man replied, "The same as each other." This is about as intelligent as much that passes for Christian faith in this religious world in which we live.

The opening verse of Hebrews 11 describes and defines faith. The preliminary definition must be understood. The following examples illustrate it. The key is furnished in verse 27, ". . . as seeing him who is invisible." Faith apprehends, as a real fact, what is not revealed to the natural senses. Faith is conviction of things when they are not seen—giving substance to things hoped for. Do not overlook the meaning of the two words, *substance* and *evidence*. The word *substance* is made up of two Greek words meaning, "that which stands under a foundation." Thus, it speaks of the ground on which one builds hope. It stands for the whole body of documents bearing on the ownership of a person's property, forming the evidence of ownership. This translation has been suggested, "Faith is a title deed of things hoped for." The Holy Spirit energized act of faith, that is exercised on the Lord Jesus, is the title deed which God places in the believer's hand, guaranteeing him possession of the thing for which he trusted. The word *evidence* means "a proof of that by which a thing is proved or tested." It means being convinced. It is not, therefore, a feebly grounded hypothesis; but a conviction put to the test—as when Noah built the ark. Saving faith is not just a mental assent to certain propositions; it reaches the heart.

Today there is a kind of unbelieving believing which is very common. Many say they trust Jesus Christ, yet they never serve Him. Many persons will readily affirm that Christ rose from the grave, but they live as though He were dead. Many will admit belief in a coming judgment day, yet they live as though they were wholly unaccountable to a holy and righteous God. It is a striking reflection that there are no atheists among the devils. They know too much to have ever succumbed to that delusion. "The devils believe and tremble" (Jas. 2:19). But why? Because these creatures believe not only in God's existence, but also in His power and absolute sovereignty. Faith which saves the soul is the kind that has confidence in Jesus Christ as sin Bearer, Deliverer, Teacher, Master, Guide, and Divine Lord. The person who has been regenerated by the Spirit of God possesses a living faith. Thus he believes on Christ. This means that Christ is the Object of faith, its living Goal, its magnet. Faith is always in motion toward Christ. Although we have already come, we are at the same time ever coming—"To whom coming . . ." (I Pet. 2:4).

There is nothing static in true faith. Each grace is a living movement granted to the regenerated person by God; therefore, the Lord Jesus is the living magnetic center Who draws the regenerated into His fellowship by His Spirit and word. The regenerated person who possesses the faculty of faith believes in Christ (Col. 1:4). This means that Christ is the sphere of the believer's spiritual life. He surrounds him on all sides. Hence, what water is to fish and air is to man, Christ is to the soul of the believer. The person who has been regenerated believes on (upon) Christ (Acts 16:31). Jesus Christ is the foundation of the life of faith. It is upon this eternal foundation, by the power of the Spirit, the structure of faith is built. Paul said, "For the which cause I also suffer these things: nevertheless I am not ashamed: for I know whom I have believed, and am persuaded that he is able to keep that which I have committed unto him against that day" (II Tim. 1:12). Here, the word *faith* is joined to the Person trusted, not only the goal, the sphere, the supporting basis; but Jesus Christ is the Person in Whom faith centers.

CONCLUSION

As we bring our studies on Regeneration and Conversion to a close, I must warn about a relatively new theory that is being proclaimed to the religious public. This theory has gained wide acceptance. The view is based upon a few texts of Scripture, whose scope is confined to the people of God. The belief has been erroneously misapplied to mean that at the cross the sin question was fully and finally settled; that all the sins of all men were laid upon the crucified Christ. This opinion affirms that Jesus Christ did as much for those who would not believe as He did for those who will believe. Thus, those who hold this idea advocate that the single issue between Christ and sinners is not the sin question, but the Son question. This is another product of this twentieth century liberalism. I shall now show the folly of this theory. (1) Unbelief is a sin. If all the sins of all men were laid on Jesus Christ, then the sin of unbelief was laid on Him. If unbelief is a sin and Christ did not suffer the penalty of it, then all sin was not laid on the Lord Jesus Christ. Would this not limit the atonement to believers? One must not forget that the power of unbelief resides in a man's depraved condition. (2) Christ said, "Ye shall die in your sins" (John 8:21,24). The Lord was speaking of that which lay on the other side of His death and resurrection. Christ did not bear these sins. Notice it says *sins*, not sin. The Jews did not seek Christ where they might find Him. They did not seek the suffering Saviour; so Christ said, "Whither I go ye cannot come." He ascended to heaven, but they could not go to heaven apart from Christ. (3) The dead shall be judged according to their works (Rev. 20:12). If the only issue between God and sinners is their attitude toward Christ; if the only ground of condemnation is rejection of the Saviour, then it would be meaningless to arraign them for their works. (4) There will be degrees of punishment (Matt. 11:22; Mark 12:40; Heb. 10:28,29). If all the sins of all men were laid on Christ, how could there possibly be any degrees of punishment for the lost? (5) The unevangelized have not heard of Christ. Not having heard of Him, they could not be charged with rejecting Him, that is, if all the sins of all men were laid upon Christ. If this were true, then John 14:6 would be false. The unbeliever is condemned in Adam, but he incurs new condemnation after he hears the truth of the gospel.

Only the hopelessly lost know what salvation delivers from; only the saved in heaven know what the salvation of God delivers to. Even they know these things imperfectly. Eternity will ever be disclosing new horrors in hell and new glories in heaven. Unbelief is twofold: negative and positive. *Negative,* is the unbelief of heathen who have never heard the gospel. How can they believe in him of whom they have not heard? *Positive,* is the sin of those who sit under the sound of the gospel, but make light of it and think it is foolishness. Thus, they incur new condemnation (Heb. 10:28,29).

If you profess to be a Christian, ask yourself if regeneration preceded your conversion. Regeneration must precede conversion in the Divine order.